# RELATIONSHIP
# OF ESTEEM VALUES
# WITH INTELLIGENCE QUOTIENT
# AND GRADE POINT AVERAGES

By: JAMES W. SIMMONS

San Francisco, California
1977

Published by

R&E RESEARCH ASSOCIATES, INC.
4843 Mission Street
San Francisco, California 94112

Publishers
Robert D. Reed and Adam S. Eterovich

Library of Congress Card Catalog Number
76-24726



I.S.B.N.
0-88247-427-8

# ACKNOWLEDGEMENT

The writer wishes to express his appreciation to the following persons for services rendered during the completion of this study:

Dr. Albert Billig, Laurence University, who served in the initial stage as Advisor; Dr. Clair T. Blikre, President of North Dakota State School of Science, for his helpful comments and suggestions as Advisor; Dr. Raymond C. Doane, Laurence University, for a thorough reading of the first draft; Dr. Thanumalaya Pillai, Department of Science and Mathematics, Mississippi Valley State University, for computerizing the data submitted in this study; Mrs. Carlee Bailey, Administrative Assistant for Special Programs and Miss Doris Jackson, Secretary to the Vice-President, at Mississippi Valley State University, Itta Bena, Mississippi, who assisted in typing the manuscript; and to the many others who were helpful in various ways, the writer is most grateful.

# TABLE OF CONTENTS

LIST OF TABLES

# CHAPTER I

## THE PROBLEM AND ITS COMPONENT PARTS

### INTRODUCTION

> In the broadest outline, American society is characterized by a
> basic moral orientation, involving emphasis on active, instru-
> mental mastery of the world in accordance with universalistic
> standards of performance.  It is a pluralistic system in which
> it is not easy to secure unitary commitment to collective
> goals.[1]

> ...whole cultures are sometimes characterized by values that
> reinforce each other and affect varied kinds of behavior.[2]

There are many problems that beset us in our modern ways of thinking and
living.  Many of those problems stem from our youth in high schools and colleges.  It
is not unusual for these youth to attack the cherished beliefs, customs, and traditions
that have permeated our society throughout the centuries.  Yet, very few teachers think
in terms of the underlying motives, concepts, or values imbedded within these youth
that cause them to act or respond in a manner that may not be acceptable in our mores.
It is at this point of origin where this study begins to probe into the nature of the
situation and the availability of the research tools and the subjects, the participating students.  It is the intention that information revealed will indicate values one
holds in esteem as well as his pattern of behavior.

It is further anticipated that such information revealed in this study will
enhance a better working relationship and understanding between youth and adult.

This study was conducted because there is an element in student learning
that is associated with the values that they hold in esteem.  In the past, teachers
have established patterns for students to follow.  As a result, many problems of conflicts and confusion existed.  The established patterns coincided with the traditional
system of education that was in operation in the United States during the early part
of the twentieth century.  Students were expected to be submissive, obedient to authority, and accept what was handed down to them by word of mouth.  With a shift in

emphasis from the traditional system in education to modern methods, students assumed a greater responsibility in helping to plan the educational program; they exercised a greater degree of freedom of expressions, and their concept of "individualism" brought about variations in attitudes and ideals. These changes in attitudes and behavior brought such an impact upon the philosophy of the traditional school system that most of its teachers failed to cope with such changes. They often blamed parents for the misconduct of their children. Most teachers held to their methods of instruction and seldom tried to determine the underlying causes of the behavior exemplified by their students.

## Background Information to the Problem

"American culture is organized around the attempt at active mastery rather than passive acceptance. It tends to be interested in the external world of things and events. It's world view tends to be open rather than closed; it emphasizes change, flux movement. In wide historical and comparative perspective, the culture places its primary faith in rationalism as opposed to traditionalism; it de-emphasizes the past and orients strongly to the future."[3]

The above quotation sets the pace for this phase of the discussion. Teachers in the past, for the most part, were ill prepared for coping with values and changes in behavior that occurred as a result of inherent values. Seldom did they take into consideration the values that students held as being a significant part of their learning experiences. They imposed values and standards upon students and expected them to be accepted without question or challenge.

In a modern society, that is dynamic and characterized by innovative methods and changes, it is essential that the teacher in modern times be prepared to consider, discover, and cope with student concepts and values that may influence their behavior. With this in mind, the researcher has examined the values held by a selected number of students to ascertain to what extent these values influence their attitudes toward learning. Although a great deal of emphasis has been placed on the theoretical value in our school system, we must consider other values that are equally important to the students, if they are to fill their places in the school's program.

2

## Statement of the Problem

<u>Major Problem</u>:  What is the relationship of esteem values held by one hundred college students of educational psychology; their intelligence quotients and grade point averages?  Selected esteem values are:  aesthetic, economic, political, religious, social, and theoretical.

<u>Subproblem</u>:  What are the theories and interpretations of the six esteem values as they relate to education?

<u>Subproblem</u>:  What is the intelligence quotient of one hundred students enrolled in educational psychology classes at the college level as measured by a standardized group test of intelligence?

<u>Subproblem</u>: What are the grade point averages of one hundred students of educational psychology?

<u>Subproblem</u>:  What are student interpretations of the six esteem values?

<u>Subproblem</u>:  What extent do students in educational psychology classes at the low intelligence quotient level relate to qualitative values?

<u>Subproblem</u>:  What extent do students in educational psychology classes at the medium intelligence quotient level relate to qualitative values?

## Purpose of the Study

The purpose of this study is to show how students of low, medium, and high level intelligence quotients relate to each of the esteem values:  aesthetic, economic, political, religious, social, and theoretical.

## Need and Significance of the Study

1.  The findings of this study will enable teachers to become cognizant of available techniques for reaching a larger number of students.

2.  The findings of this study will contribute to increased understanding of student values as a means of enhancing student-teacher relations.

3.  The findings of this study will enable teachers and others to know what

particular values students identify themselves with which may or may not be related to those held by the instructor.

4. It is anticipated that the ultimate value of the findings will be significant to teachers, administrators, and research workers who work with students in a similar capacity.

5. It is anticipated that, as a by-product, this study will reveal some information that will be pertinent to the priority value system in the educational world.

# CHAPTER II

## ASSUMPTIONS, DEFINITIONS, HYPOTHESES, AND DELIMITATIONS

### ASSUMPTIONS

It is assumed:

1. That the administration of the Otis Self-Administering Test of Mental Ability is a valid instrument for this study.

2. That the grade each participating student received in the educational psychology class represented his accumulative semester average.

3. That the primary value listed by a student represents the one that he holds in highest esteem.

4. That the responses recorded for each participating student, represent an accurate account of his performance.

5. That the values listed in this study are divided into two categories: qualitative (primary values) and quantitative (secondary values).

6. That the information received from this study concerning primary values held by students will be helpful in the teaching and learning situations.

7. That all individuals hold a variety of esteem values.

### Definitions

Intelligence Quotient is an index of an individual's development, determined by dividing his mental age by his chronological age and multiplying by 100.[4]

The mean is the arithmetic average found by adding a series of scores together and dividing by the number of cases.[5]

The median is the point on the scale which divides the total number of measures or cases into two equal groups.[6]

Standard Deviation is the square root of the sum of deviations squared by the number of cases.[7]

Validity is the degree to which a test measures what it purports to measure.

Reliability is the consistency of scores obtained by the same person when retested by identical or with an equivalent form of the test.[9]

Grade Point Average is a numerical index assigned to college students by institutions using, in this instance, A = 4.00, B = 3.00, C = 2.00, F = 0.00.

Values are a part of an individual's inner life, expressed through behavior. From this point of view, his behavior represents the best and most effective judgment he is capable of at the time he is in his immediate situation.[10]

Aesthetic - the aesthetic man seeks his highest value in form and harmony. Each experience is judged from the standpoint of grace, symmetry, or fitness. His chief interest is in the episodes of life.

Theoretical - the interest of the theoretical man is empirical, critical, and rational. He is an intellectualist, frequently a scientist or philosopher.

Economic - the economic man is utilitarian. He is thoroughly practical and conforms well to the prevailing stereotype of the average businessman.

Social - the highest value for this type is the love of people. The social man prizes other persons as ends, and is therefore himself kind, sympathetic, and un-selfish.

Political - the political man is interested in power. He wishes above all else for personal power and influence.

Religious - the religious man is mythical. He seeks to comprehend the cosmos as a whole and relates himself to its embracing totality.

Academic Assessment refers to grade point distribution, intellectual attainment, and priority values.

Esteem Values indicate preferred values, often used interchangeably with the term priority values.

Qualitative Values are designated as aesthetic, religious, and theoretical.

Quantitative Values are those values designated as economic political and social.

Primary Values are considered of major importance in comparison with other values.

Secondary Values are considered to be of minor importance in comparison with other values.

## Hypotheses

1.  There is no relationship between I.Q. scores and qualitative values.

2.  There is no relationship between I.Q. scores and quantitative values.

3.  There is no relationship between I.Q. scores and aesthetic values.

4.  There is no relationship between I.Q. scores and economic values.

5.  There is no relationship between I.Q. scores and political values.

6.  There is no relationship between I.Q. scores and religious values.

7.  There is no relationship between I.Q. scores and social values.

8.  There is no relationship between I.Q. scores and theoretical values.

## Delimitations

1.  This study is limited to the following six esteem values:  aesthetic, economic, political, religious, social and theoretical

2.  To one hundred students who were enrolled in the educational psychology classes during the school term 1971-72

3.  To the extent that only one form (A) of the Otis Self-Administering Test of Mental Ability was given to one hundred participants

4.  To the material that was available for administering, distributing, and compiling results on the students

5.  To the extent that the responses recorded and presented are accurate

6.  To the uniformity of conditions required for administering the test of Mental Ability in the classroom.

# CHAPTER III

## REVIEW OF THE RELATED LITERATURE

This chapter is designed to present a survey of the literature pertinent to the current research problem. The various facts the research studies reveal include the utilization of intelligence tests at other institutions of higher learning, the grade point averages and the grading system in relation to their transfer value to other areas of learning as well as employment situations, and the significance of the esteem values as they affect man in their theoretical and practical applications in every day life.

Information about related studies included in this chapter will be categorized as follows:

A. Tests of Intellectual Ability

B. Reliability and Validity of Intelligence Tests

C. Purposes of Intelligence Tests

D. Possibilities of Intellectual Expansion

E. Limitations of Intellectual Expansion

F. Grade Point Distribution

G. Socioeconomic Status and College Success

H. Value of Grading System

I. Cultural Values and Norms

J. The Transmission of Values

K. Delineations of the Aesthetic Value

L. The Image in Economic Value

M. Philosophical Implications of the Political Value

N. The Role of Religious Values in Life

O. An Approach to the Social Value

P. Divergent Views on the Theoretical Value

Q. Values in Relations to Education and Life

## A. Tests of Intellectual Ability

In an unpublished doctoral dissertation, Joseph Raymond Johnson reported that the Henmon Nelson Tests of Mental Ability are important criteria in assessing students' ability to succeed. He also stated that the test could be used to determine the class sections to which students will be assigned.[11]

Sanford stated that no intelligence test can be useful unless it yields a reliable measure, unless the results obtained on one occasion are essentially the same results obtained on another. It has been generally accepted that an intelligence test reported by a competent examiner using an established test, will not vary more than two or more points from the intelligence quotient reported by the same examiner using the alternative form of the test on different occasions.[12]

## B. Reliability and Validity of Intelligence Tests

The question of validity of intelligence tests is fairly intricate. On the average, the individual who behaves intelligently on a test will behave intelligently in other situations. Certain ways of behaving such as honesty, anxiety, and intelligence are validated in an indirect fashion. The extent to which an individual scores on a test, as reported by theory or less formal expectations, gives validity to the test which has separated those individuals. A test may be reliable but not valid, but a test is never valid if it is not reliable.[13]

Lewis M. Terman wrote: "The Otis Group Intelligence Test was the first scientifically grounded and satisfactory scale for testing subjects in groups, and it probably comes as near testing raw 'brain power' as any systems of tests yet devised. It is a necessity in schools, industries, armies, or any other institution in which the mental ability of human beings is a factor for consideration."

Publishers of the Otis Test stated that it is a valid measure of general mental ability. It will enable a teacher or administrator to measure the native ability of pupils in groups rapidly and accurately for the purpose of: (1) classification in regard to the native capacities to learn, (2) elimination of the feebleminded who should be placed in special institutions, (3) selection of the vocation in which the degree of mentality indicates the highest possible achievement, and (4) determination of cases of probable delinquency and proper punishment or remedial action for criminal acts.

The reliability coefficient reported is a correlation between two experimental forms of the scale. Another source of information on validity, but not labeled as such, is the table of Binet mental age equivalents which indicates a definite relationship between Otis Scores and Binet Mental Age Values.[14]

### C. Purposes of Intelligence Tests

The function of the Otis Self-Administering Test of Mental Ability has been described by Munn. He stated that intelligence tests serve two main functions: (1) for selecting those to be admitted to school and college, (2) for guidance purposes. Most students take such a test when they enter college, and their scores are filed away in the Registrar's office and the office of the Dean.

If a student makes a very low score, he may be asked to take an individual test; however, if he makes a high score on the intelligence test, his motives for attending college may be investigated.[15]

### D. Possibilities of Intellectual Expansion

Representatives of the system of modern psychology, the exponents of cognitive field theory, have emphasized that capacity for intelligent behavior is modified by learning. Its advocates do not think in terms of any limitations of intelligence. In fact, Combs and Syngg stated that the possibilities for human perception seem almost infinite. They further stated that given a health physical organism to provide the vehicle for perception, a stimulating environment, challenging and fruitful problems, and a nonrestrictive self-concept, there seems to be no end to the perceptions possible

10

to the individual. Given the proper conditions there is no reason why the measurement of intelligence should not increase during his lifetime. Old age may produce certain physiological deteriorations which may reduce the capacity for differentiating new perceptions. On the other hand, Combs and Syngg have cited numerous cases that have been reported of persons who have retained a remarkable capacity for intellectual growth and creativity until the age of 90 and beyond.[16]

## E. Limitations of Intellectual Growth

The essential ingredients for continued growth in intelligence are open-mindedness to new ideas and willingness to criticize one's most cherished convictions. For most persons the attainment of these ingredients is very difficult; their intelligence quotient, as measured by reliable known measuring devices, does not change markedly over a period of time. In the case of some persons the intelligence quotient remains stable, or may even regress. One can suppose that one's degree of openmindedness and one's ability for self-criticism are largely a function of his education.[17]

## F. Grade Point Distribution

In a study conducted in 1959 of 180 publicly supported institutions accredited by the National Council for Accreditation of Teacher Education (NCATE), Magee found variations in scholarship requirements for the admission to upper-level professional work. Sixteen percent of the colleges used only the admission to Teacher Education that required better than 2.00 (C) scholarship average in the total program or in specified areas. Eighty percent of all institutions reporting considered a 2.00 (C) grade point adequate for admission to a program leading to certification. Only 19.5 percent of the institutions required a grade point average above (C) in any part of the candidate's program.

The required grade point averages above 2.00 prevailed in 11 of 35 institutions. The requirements applied only to the major field and to professional courses in two institutions; they applied only to students preparing for secondary school

11

teaching, and in 19 institutions they applied only to the total college work completed.

The total grade point average seems to be the consensus as the best criterion used at the time of admission to teacher education. In analyzing the data in this study, one researcher found that of 24 students who were rated below average in teaching success, 7 were admitted with grade point averages below 2.3, 12 were admitted with a grade point average between 2.3 and 2.5, while 4 had grade point averages of above 3.00. He found that if the minimal grade point averages were increased to 2.5, 13 of the 24 below average teachers would have been rejected, 3 of the average, 7 of the above average, and 1 of the superior teachers would have been rejected.[18]

## G.  Socioeconomic Status and College Success

Hill[19] and Bond[20] stated that social standing or wealth were key items in terms of college success. Hill said that it is well-known that a relationship exists between socioeconomic class and scholastic success. Bond believed that whenever standardized tests are applied, the scores range themselves according to the wealth or poverty of the population concerned; this is the situation where rural may be compared with urban or one geographical region can be compared with another.

Witty and Bloom said, "Encouragement and guidance are required...by gifted students in college in order that they will develop fully."[21]

Terman concluded that the highly endowed mentally differ from the average in degree rather than in kind of intelligence.[22]

Hollingshead stated that we ought not to let ourselves get so bemused with the importance of developing genius that we neglect those just below them in ability, for those just below have an almost equally important contribution to make, mostly in the direction of developing, explaining, and diffusing the thoughts of those who are in the very top rank.[23]

## H.  Value of Grading System

The value of a grading system to the student depends on the way he perceives the results. If his perception is in accord with the grade the teacher assigns, seeking a grade may promote learning. This situation is more likely to be true in the case of a student of high ability who has had a successful past. When a low grade is assigned, diagnosis of difficulties should follow. The assignment of a grade provides a progress report to the student. This report acts as a feedback in rewarding good efforts, or in showing that a little more effort is required.[24]

Each individual comes to attach significant meanings to certain experiences and to avoid or reject others.[25] No single grade should mean so much, but in student teaching it does, and its effect can be detrimental. A grade of "C" on campus may be gracefully accepted, even by the bright student, for it is easily absorbed within the cumulative grade point. This evaluation is not true for the grade of "C" in student teaching because student teaching is a culminating activity. It stands out stark and unyielding for all public personnel to see. Although it is supposed to indicate average abilities, it can and frequently does represent dead-end to professional aspirations. It is little wonder that supervisors award it only after considerable soul searching. The use of letter grades tends to interfere with the good relationship that should exist between the student, his college or university supervisor, and supervising teacher.[26]

One researcher stated that nothing can be efficiently learned other than through parroting or brute training unless it meets needs, desires, curiosity, or fantasy. He further stated that teachers should teach what they consider important--which is all that they can skillfully teach anyway. Such a view holds major implications concerning the coming together of educational technology and teacher individualism.[27]

Using the chi-square test of independence, Tikalsky found statistically significant relationships between values and theory orientation. He also found significant relationship in philosophical orientation and values. The sample also showed a general tendency toward liberal orientation with respect to political, economic, personal, moral, and religious issues.[28]

## I. Cultural Values and Norms

A value is anything that is prized or of benefit. Values do not consist in desires but rather the desirable, that is, what we not only want but feel that it is right and proper to want for ourselves and others. Values are abstract standards that transcend the impulses of the moment and ephemeral situations. A cultural value may be defined as a widely held belief or sentiment that some activities, relationships, or goals are important to the community's identity or well-being. They are often held unconsciously or expressed as themes cutting across a variety of specific attitudes. The values of a people are not immediately apparent.

The academic motivation of disadvantaged students in a special community college program was compared to that of regular matriculants.[29] In addition, multiple regression analyses were made of measures of ability and several other personality characteristics as predictors of academic success for special program students. While the groups did not differ in motivation, somewhat different patterns emerged. Regular matriculants were more concerned with social evaluation and special students with self-worth. Predictors most similar to activities required for successful college performance were those most highly correlated with the criteria: high school average, Otis I.Q., study habits and attitudes, and reality of aspiration were the best predictors.

In designing a new program at an institution of higher learning, Patricia S. Plant stated that undergraduate education is intimately related to values which students are attempting to form, and that the issues which they must confront are perennial issues of morals, politics, and aesthetics. She further stated that the psychic involvement of man is real and it is as important to understand as man's scientific and technological progress.[30]

Values reflect the culture of a society and are widely shared by the members of the culture. They are often expressed in terms of what is desirable or "good" or what ought to be. For example, the typical American values human equality; the typical lawyer believes in "due process;" the typical physician holds health to be desirable, while the typical teacher entertains the idea that intellectual competence is an "ought to be." Values are both positive and negative; the positive values are the "desirables;" the negative values are the "undesirables." If an individual accepts a value for himself, it may become a goal for him.

Krech and his associates stated that at least four sets of important factors determine the acceptable level of achievement of these goals. In the first place, the individual's understanding of his capacities and limitations helps set these levels. The man who sets as his goal success as a scholar, but thinks of himself as possessing only a "fair" intellect, will not seek to become a top scholar in his field. He will feel that he has realized his goal when he is accepted as merely another scholar among the vast company of scholars.

A second factor is the awareness of what levels of achievement are possible. A man who values economy and believes that no man ever amassed more than a home and several acres of land will accept a much lower level of achievement as "success" than will be cosmopolite who knows that others have amassed millions of dollars in wealth.

The third factor is an experiential one, the individual's own history of success and failure. The chronically successful man will demand of himself "successful;" the chronically failing man will progressively reduce his level in order to defend himself against further failures.

The fourth factor is the social factor, the status of the individual in his group. An evaluation of the self, like any other evaluation, requires a comparison with something else. In the judgment of the self, the "something else" consists of comparative reference individuals and reference groups. In Hyman's pioneering study of subjective status, the individual's conception of his own position relative to others, he found that the individual's evaluation of himself is primarily determined by his perception of his relative position or standing in two different reference groups: (1) membership groups, and (2) a group in which he aspires to membership. A premedical student may evaluate his intelligence by comparing himself with his fellow students (a membership group). At other times, he may evaluate his intelligence by comparing himself with "great physicians," (a group to which he aspires to belong).[31]

What one has learned is ultimately the best to help him discover what he ought to do, and to find out who and what he is. The path to ethical and value decisions, to wiser choices is by the way of the discovery of facts, truth, reality, and the nature of the particular person. The more he knows about his own nature, his deep wishes, his temperament, his constitution, what he seeks and yearns for and what really satisfies him, the more effortless, automatic, and epiphenomenal become his value choices. Many problems simply disappear; many others are easily solved by knowing what is in conformity with one's nature, and what is suitable and right.[32]

Young people do not assimilate the values of their group by learning the words (truth and justice). They learn attitudes, habits, and ways of judging. They learn these in intense transactions with their immediate family or associates; they learn them in the routines and crises of living. They do not learn ethical principles; they emulate ethical (or unethical) people. They do not analyze or list the attributes they wish to develop; they identify with people who seem to have these attributes. For these reasons young people need models, both in their imaginative life and in their environment, models of what man at his best can be.[33]

Cultural norms are based on cultural values. They are guides to conduct, specifying what is appropriate or inappropriate, setting limits within which individuals may seek alternate ways to achieve their goals. Norms are usually framed as rules, prescriptions, or standards to be followed by people who occupy specified roles.[34]

## J.  The Transmission of Values

Perhaps the best way to transmit values is to create an atmosphere on campus.[35] The best environment for the development of character is the result of unity in common goals, a complicated tradition to which all phases of campus life makes their particular contribution.

Arsenian used the Study of Values to assess changes in attitudes during four years of college. He noted some statistically significant changes over the four year period, especially the emphasis placed on religious beliefs. According to his study, the shift was apparently away from religious to other value orientations.[36]

Allport and Vernon developed a value inventory called the "Study of Values," designed to measure dominant interest in personality. It was originally published in 1931, and revised in 1951 and 1960. It gives a measure of relative importance that an individual places on theoretical, economic, aesthetic, social, political, and religious values. Individuals are given the same total scores. Differences are in terms of the relative emphasis the individual puts on the six areas. This method of scoring makes it a useful device for showing different assessments of changes in emphases.[37]

Every teacher observes and must be prepared to cope with behavior indicative of some inadequacy in value orientation. Each time an incidence of this type occurs, the teacher must strive to understand its meaning from the standpoint of development of social attitudes and to implement corrective procedures to produce broader educational gains. Procedures designed only to eliminate specific behavior, without regard to its fuller meaning and the effect on the student's value of orientation in general, may well result in the reinforcement of less mature behavior forms.[38]

### K. Delineations of the Aesthetic Value

Aesthetics is a philosophy of fine arts in its relation to beauty. The domain of art is the expression of Spirit in sensuous form. This definition of aesthetic value indicates the range and limitations of art. The development of the fine arts proceeds from abstract inadequacy to a more harmonious relation of Spirit and sensuous form in which it is expressed, and then to transcendence of the form by growing depth or scope of the meaning that seeks expression.

In the pursuit of beauty as in the quest for truth or goodness, there are three aspects of perfection in ideal interplay: (1) aesthetic beauty, (2) sensuous perception of beauty, and (3) aesthetic contemplation. Aesthetic beauty is the beauty of sensuous perception. The object which is beautiful to see and the lovely harmony are not to be explained as merely shapely or symmetrical. We find an object of sense

17

beautiful because in it we experience sensuously a certain adumbration of spiritual meaning. "The material thing becomes beautiful by communicating in the thought that flows from the Divine. Harmonies unheard create the harmonies we hear and wake the soul to consciousness of beauty."[39]

From sensuous perception of beauty, the soul can rise to loftier admiration for ideal objects. It can behold the "beautiful beyond the beauty of the evening and the dawn;" it can behold "the God-like splendor of virtue...the perfect goodness established in stainless shrine." Aesthetic contemplation, as interpreted by Plotinus, traverses art and enters morality, philosophy, and religion. It is one side of the pathway to perfection, while moral activity is another side.[40]

## L.   The Image in Economic Value

Even in the simplest theories of economic values, the concept of an image is latent. Economics is the study of mankind in the ordinary business of life; it examines that part of individual and social action which is most closely connected with the attainment and with the use of the material requisites of well-being.[41] Economic behavior is conceived as a process of "maximization." Economic man is supposed to be capable of at least three processes involving an image. In the first place he is conscious of the alternatives which lie before him. His image consists of a complex relational image of form, "If I do A, then B, C, D, will follow." Or in the simplest form, we suppose his mind to be like a department store full of commodities, each with a convenient price ticket attached.

In addition to the image of the alternatives, economic man is also likely to be able to give value-ordering to all relevant alternatives, that is, to all parts of this image. Not only do the combinations of his mental department store have price tags. What is even more astonishing, all combinations of commodities have utility tags.

His final task, after his imagination has performed these Herculean tasks, is a simple one. All he needs to do is to scan all possible combinations which are open to him and all of his alternative acts, rank them in order on the parade ground of value, and pick out the top of the class. This process of the best alternative is what is known as "maximization," around which a considerable amount of theory is built. The fact that the whole range of alternatives is to come not with utility tags but with profit tags, makes it presumably easier to detect that combination which has the largest profit tag than it is to find the combination with the highest utility.[42]

## M.  Philosophical Implications of the Political Values

Just as the traditional subject matter of economics is wealth in terms of that is, commodities, the traditional subject matter of the political value is power. The political process may be abstracted from the general processes of social life by concentrating on the processes by which decisions are made. We are not only interested in how decisions are made, but who makes them.

It is customary to think of the structure of organizations in terms of authoritarian system. We have a strict hierarchy of roles. Each role contains the expectation of subordination to higher roles, and is transmitted to the lower roles as orders. The lower roles are expected to execute the orders without questioning. All decisions originate at the top and are transmitted downwards, where they are supposed to be delineated in acts. The information which ascends the role structure should be feedback from these acts. The form of information is governed from above and not from below. It is not volunteered, it is requested.

At the other end of the scale, we have the democratic organization. Authority is now designed to proceed from below. The higher roles should act on behalf of and to be responsible to the lower roles. What this means in practice is that the decisions of the higher roles have to be made by discussion. As a result of these feedbacks, the decisions are modified until substantial agreement is reached. The discussion proceeds until the higher roles announce the decision which receives the approval of the lower ones or at least a majority of them. The dynamics of political life can be interpreted largely in terms of the interaction of two processes. The first is the process whereby political images are created and distributed among individuals of a society. The second is a process whereby specialized skills and knowledge are distributed among the people of the society.[43]

### N.  The Role of Religious Values in Life

Bertocci, a philosopher, defines religion as follows:  "The essence or core of  religion is the personal belief that one's most important values are sponsored by, or in harmony with, the enduring structure of the universe, whether they are sponsored by society or not."[44]

In the religious experience we do not argue ourselves into believing that our value commitments have the support of the cosmos.  On the contrary, in the moment of religious experience, it is immediately felt that a power greater than our own is on the scene and is playing a leading role in the drama of values.  Without this feeling, prayer, communion or worship of any sort are empty rituals.

One feature of religious experience is to see and feel ourselves, others, nature and the cosmos in dramatic terms.  There is a plot and there are characters; there is a conflict between good and evil forces; the ultimate outcome is never in doubt; the immediate one is the only one in doubt.  The world is understood historic-ally as a story of a plot, conflict, and prediction.  The religious experience is social in that it feels the powers of the universe as fellow actors in the drama; it is also moral because the drama is a conflict of choice between good and evil.  It is intellectual because the drama has a plot that must be understood for the religious feeling to take place.

There are those who hold that while religious experiences may help people to become more courageous, more confident, more humble, and more moral, the lasting value of dignity and worth lies in the intrinsic phase, the feeling itself.  In spite of the various views and values man attach to religion, it is certain that the religious ex-perience does precisely what a conceptual experience cannot do  It gives an intense

certainty and vivid awareness of a power that is on the side of righteousness and
goodness.[45]

## O.  An Approach to the Social Value

The social values of man are always governed by two trends:  one toward stability and security, and the other toward adventure, exploration of the unknown, and
creation.  The trend toward security is the manifestation of self-preservation which
we define today more precisely as the homeostatic principle.  It is expressed in man's
striving to secure the basic necessities for survival with a minimum expenditure of
energy.  The trend toward new ventures into the unknown is the manifestation of an
equally basic biological principle, that of growth and propagation.  Neither of these
two trends is more fundamental than the other.  They both constitute life's activities.
Growth and propagation result from the surplus which remains over and above what is
needed to survive.  Whatever is left of that amount which is needed for maintaining
the homeostatic equilibrium is retained in the form of creativity--both biological and
social.  A great deal of this surplus is discharged playfully or for the sake of meeting the challenge of obstacles in adventurous pursuit.  Both motives, the quest for
security and the lust for adventure and mastery, are always present in the social
aspirations of man.[47]

## P.  Divergent Views of the Theoretical Values

The theoretical values are frequently referred to as the values concerning
knowledge.  Most philosophers divide the "theory of knowledge" into two categories:
(1) epistemology, and (2) logic.  Epistemology is the study of the nature of knowledge
and the process of knowing.  Logic is the study of the methods of deriving knowledge
from preexisting knowledge, and of the criteria of validity in reasoning.

Heraclitus believed in the ideas that he formed with the mind rather than in
the information given to him by his senses.  Essentially, this method is known as
idealism, which contends that the world which we have before us is in the fullest sense

real and true.  One of the major problems of human knowledge is the curious relationship between the direct and vivid impacts of our senses which often mislead us, and
the indirect toilsome inferences of our reason in which we alone ultimately seem to
trust.

Socrates held that virtue and knowledge were the same.  He stated that a
man who knows what is right will do it; no man chooses evil as such.

Plato attained a general theory of knowledge in terms of reasons.  According
to him, sensory perception can give us only unstable impressions of particulars.

One of the principal aspects of Aristotle's philosophy is gnosiology, an
experimental scheme in which all knowledge is developed from sense impressions, and
embraced in the categories of substance, quantity, quality, relation, place, time,
posture, possession, action, and passion.[48]

Melvil Dewey divided all knowledge into ten main classes, which is known as
the Dewey Decimal System.  Since a great deal of research and references are housed
in the libraries throughout the country, one's understanding of this classification
will enable him to locate any branch of knowledge in which he is interested, in the
most expedient fashion.

### Q.  Values in Relation to Education and Life

There is increasing attention to determining the purposes of education by
locating the values to which educational purposes might contribute.  Professional people have long been evasive about values because of social pressures, but they have
found that values cannot be escaped and many of them have decided to deal with them
consciously and directly.  One advantage of this approach is that the esteem values
have been with us a long time and are likely to remain, so that educational policies
and programs attached to these values are unlikely to change to the extent that they
have been vacillating when lesser guides have been used.[49]

Clyde Kluckhohn, a distinguished anthropologist, said:  "From primitive tribes to Egypt, China, Greece, and the Christian world in its flower, the task of education has been first and foremost that of transmitting, expounding, and in some cases refining the great values of each culture. The teaching of information and skills, until recently, has been essentially little more than a means to the more ultimate end."[50]

Values determine what everyone connected with education will do: students, parents, teachers, administrators, and members of boards of education. All activities in a school system are chaotic until there is some reconciliation of values. It has been stated that the pursuit of these esteem values, more or less unconscious, holds American society and the American educational system together. What is needed is more conscious attention to these values. The esteem values should be sought and their implications currently known should be deliberately spelled out in education.

The central democratic concept about which all other values coalesce is that individuals have personal worth and dignity and must always be considered as ends of the continuum means to the end. The best total development of every member of our society becomes the overall goal of education. Every arrangement and practice can be tested as means of working toward that goal. There is a whole constellation of related concepts of values that may guide our efforts in the educational process. There is no shortage of esteem values; the shortage is in applying them systematically to education.[51]

Theodore Brameld in his book, <u>Ends and Means in Education</u> gave a list of human needs that are universal and applicable to the esteem values. He states: Most men do not want chronic insecurity; they cherish the value of steady work, and steady income. Most men do not want drudgery, monotony or routine; they cherish the value of novelty, adventure, and creativity. Most men do not want ignorance, they cherish the value of knowledge, information, and skill.

Most men do not want continual domination; they cherish the value of participation, and sharing. Most men do not want loneliness; they cherish the value of

23

companionship, mutual devotion, and belongingness. Most men do not want bewilderment; they cherish the value of fairly immediate meaning, significance, order, and direction.[52]

We are going to be more cognizant of esteem values and their decisive place in education and in life. We shall find greater agreement than we now have regarding the values the schools should uphold. Having fixed our eyes on the highest attainable values, we shall be able to determine more soundly the needs of individuals that call for education. With needs established, educational objectives and purposes can be clearer in the minds of all, and particularly in the minds of students, whose purpose in undergoing education is all-important. With values, needs, and purposes better known, more accurate estimates of the development of individual students and of the contributions of the schools to respond will be possible.[53]

### R.   Research Studies Pertinent to Values Held by College Students

A guide for teaching values in social studies takes a positive stand with regard to the importance of values...based on the belief that many personal and societal problems are the results of unsolved conflicts in values. It is hypothesized that students who have continuing experiences in value identification are better able to meet the problems of daily life than those who lack such experiences, and that the social studies offer an effective vehicle for value classification as its content is drawn from the world of relationships and interactions. As a means of obtaining this goal, activities involve entire classes, small groups, and individuals as well as student-teacher and peer interaction related to social studies content areas.[54]

Forty University of Toledo Teacher Corps interns (23 black and 17 white) were asked to respond to a Rokeach Value Survey on the first day of regular classes, at the end of the year, and at the end of the program. The objective was to examine what significant value changes, if any, took place during the program. Results were assessed according to racial groups rather than individuals. Results of the first survey showed that the black interns were more concerned with cleanliness, indepen-dence, politeness, and self-control than were white interns. White interns were

24

more concerned with honesty and salvation than blacks. Results of the second survey showed that the groups differed significantly only in their ranking of the value "clean." Survey data at the end of the program indicate that blacks and whites demonstrate fewer significant differences in their values. The author concluded that experiential influences rather than racial ones may be dominant in affecting value formation, attitudes and behavior.[55]

One of the goals of the social studies is to help students gain and refine skills in the area of value clarification. Value sheets, carefully planned activities designed to elicit value clarifying patterns of language from students are one way of securing value clarification. Sheets planned in conjunction with ongoing units of instruction, avoid isolating the process of valuing from its important content. Five different formats - standard forced-choice, affirmative, rank order, classification and criterion-represent different demands in valuing, from learning to express and share values to identifying a basis for decision making, inventing solutions, organizing solutions, organizing preferences hierarchially, linking choices with consequence, and recognizing the relationships among choices, social policies, decision making grounds, and consequences. Two examples for each format indicate some ways that context can be chosen from social studies materials. Each of the value sheets contains the social studies and scientific context of a situation to which a student reacts or in which a student participates as well as questions in the form of discussion starter.[56]

A need existed to develop a graphic procedure to predict student success in a 2-year engineering technology program at Kent State University, based on ACT scores and high school grades. The study stemmed from the need to help students identify their chances of success, to help clarify their goals, and to help indicate needed institutional responses. Regression analysis determined how well college achievement correlated with a composite high school grades and ACT scores. Records of 48 students from September, 1970 through June, 1973 provided the data. The analysis resulted in a coefficient correlation $r$ = .85 to provide a fairly high predictive measure. The report illustrates a reliable means of objectively predicting student success based on ACT scores and high school grades.[57]

In a longitudinal study of student performance at Harper College, a sample of full-time and part-time students who enrolled at the College in the fall semesters during the years 1967 through 1972 was studied. The results of the study showed that in 1969 and 1970 more students were leaving before they accumulated 15 hours credit, and fewer were completing the College's programs. The trend was reversed in later years, with students persisting at higher levels. The average GPA of students was higher in the last three years than in any of the previous three years. The factor affecting GPA most was age, with students 21 and over earning half a grade point average higher than those students under 21 years of age. In addition, students enrolled in career courses earned about one-fifth of a grade point higher than did those in baccalaureate oriented courses.[58]

This study describes an intensive teacher training program of ten weeks for minority group college graduates at Boston State College, prior to teaching in the public schools. The Personal Orientation Inventory and the Minnesota Teacher Attitude Inventory were used as pre- and post-training measures to assess attitudes and values of the College graduate into ones more congruent with good teaching and self-actualization. Also the program seems to have been more successful with those trainees going into secondary rather than elementary education.[59]

The Questionnaire on Student Attitude Toward Economics (QSATE-O) was administered as a pretest in the first week of classes to the students enrolled in seven sections of Economics 101 at Ohio University. The purposes of this study were to obtain measures of student attitude toward economics at the beginning and at the end of introductory courses, and to estimate the direction as well as the extent of changes in attitude over the time period when students were enrolled in the course. Among the major findings are the following: (1) student attitude toward economics tended to deteriorate over the time period when the students were enrolled in the course, and (2) the demand for economic knowledge and instruction in economics was lower at the conclusion of the course, than at the beginning. To determine whether the QSATE-O was valid for the population of students with whom it was used, a predictive validity problem was constructed and tested. The reliability of the instrument was also measured. Results indicate that the instrument was a valid measure of student attitude and that it operated in a highly reliable manner. The original and revised forms of the questionnaire on student attitude toward economics and a summary of statistical procedures used in the study are included in the report.[60]

This study provides information on the current practice of grading, recording, and averaging. Five hundred forty-four institutions of higher education returned a survey form, a 73 percent return. Two and four year institutions, public and private, in all states were included in the survey. Conclusions suggest: (1) institutions in higher education are experimenting with a wide variety of practices, and these experiments are causing much distress to some registrars, professors, and deans; (2) there are many different types of grading systems as there are institutions; (3) most of the responding institutions use one or more types of non-traditional grades, but few use them exclusively. The prevalent practice reported by most institutions is to use non-traditional grades in courses outside the major and to allow student option; (4) there is a trend toward being less punitive with grades in institutions of higher education; and (5) as competency-based education becomes more widespread in higher education, it appears that additional modification and changes in grading, recording and averaging practices will come into being and that the traditional transcript/GPA approach will lose its historical meaning.[61]

This study describes the value of life change as a non-intellectual predictor of college grades. A correlation was sought between the amount of change experienced and grade point average (GPA) accumulated by students during their freshmen year. Three hundred freshmen were evenly divided into low, medium and high academic risk groups as indicated by college entrance examinations. Fisher's t-test on life change totals revealed that low GPA subjects in each group had experienced significantly greater amounts of change. Significant levels were .05 for low risk groups and .01

for the medium and high risk groups. These results indicate that life change warrants additional study and holds promise of being a nonintellectual variable with which to supplement existing methods of predicting college grades.[62]

To give teachers help in understanding themselves better and in relating more positively to their students, small discussion groups were organized to provide maximum opportunities for teachers to express thoughts and feelings about themselves and about problems they were facing in the classroom that prevented them from relating positively to their students. Through group dynamics, the teachers gained support from relating positively to their students. Through group dynamics, the teachers gained support from each other as they helped each other solve problems. A comparison of the pre-test and post-test scores on the Minnesota Teachers Attitude Inventory revealed significantly changed scores in a positive direction for teachers who participated in this learning experience.[63]

This study is a secondary analysis of data from recent surveys of faculty and students in 89 American colleges and universities. It explores undergraduate socialization in academic departments, focusing on the impact of student and faculty norms concerning the desirability of liberal vs. vocational education as outcomes of college, and primary social interaction among faculty and students. An analysis of covariance was used to investigate five values similar to those in the Cornell Value Study. The findings indicate that departmental faculty contact is more consistently influential than peer ties, having similar, positive effects for both sexes on three of the five values - helping others, creativity, and career eminence. This suggests lower salience on peer influences in departments relative to other college settings. Educational norms, while not as important as primary interaction, are more influential for men than for women. When the joint effects of norms and social relationships are examined, faculty contacts continue to be the most influential variable, regardless of norms. Only for women's creativity orientation is the strong influence reduced by peer ties, regardless of those peer norms. Findings are interpreted with respect to differential styles, by sex of organizational behavior and their implications for undergraduate socialization.[64]

Depressed and nondepressed college students were frustrated in an incentive task utilizing a non-reward technique. Matched controls undertook a similar task in which a frustration condition was absent. Subjects were 127 undergraduate psychology students. Pre-test and post-test measures of hostility and depression were obtained. The Beck Depression Inventory, the Hostility and Depression Scales of the Today Form of the Multiple Affect Adjective Check List and the Digit Symbol subtest of the Wechsler Adult Intelligence Scale were used as measures. It was found that frustration increased both depression and hostility in the nondepressed subjects. The findings suggest that there is a significant positive correlation between depression and hostility.[65]

In a search for the eternal verities, the role of man in a world of dynamite and confusion is constantly changing. His development is comparable to that of life within a shell. As he reaches a culminating point based on training and previous experience, he breaks within this shell and comes into contact with life in a new environment, consisting of new experiences. Man's ability to adapt, to create, to fashion images enables him to reach into the supersensuous realm of ideas. This transcendental flight enables him to identify himself with a world of the unknown--an object bigger than himself. Thus, he conceives himself as a distinct entity--one that separates him from that of an infrahuman. This uniqueness places him into the category of a human being. Man lives in a perpetual world of facts and fancy, reality and imagination, consisting of values classified as primary and secondary. As a part of this ever growing process, man must continue to ascertain, identify, and select those values which have meaning to him. In order that he may maintain his strategic position, he must be able to sift the grains of truth from that of falsity, discover the whole from that of parts, and sense the values that have meaning from those that are meaningless. Then he should be able to lead a life that is most valuable for himself and for the society in which he lives.

## Summary

Some of the tests that have been used in identifying effective teachers are: Miller Analogies Tests, National Teacher Examinations, and the Otis Self-Administering Test of Mental Ability. Research has revealed that the Henmon Nelson Tests of Mental Ability are important criteria in assessing students' ability to succeed in school work.

The criteria for the establishment of intelligence tests are: reliability, validity, objectivity, and standardization. Intelligence tests are best interpreted in terms of percentile rank. Intelligence tests are used in school for two main purposes: (1) to select those who will be admitted, and (2) to be utilized for guidance purposes.

Research reveals that most institutions accept grade point averages of 2.00 (C) for admission to teacher education programs leading to certification. However, there were instances where above average grades were required for one's major field. The total grade point average seems to be the best criterion used at the time of admission to teacher education.

Perhaps the best way to transmit values is to create an atmosphere on campus. Research shows that in a study of values a shift in emphasis occurs during a four-year period. Investigators have noted that individuals have placed a measure of relative importance on aesthetic, economic, political, religious, social, and theoretical values.

The aesthetic values focused attention upon the beauty as expressed in the fine arts. They enable man to appreciate and interpret what he sees in terms of perfection, form, and symbols that coincide with the nature of the works of art.

The economic values attach significance to that part of individual and social action which is most closely connected with the attainment and use of material requisites of well-being. They place an economic tag and a utility tag on commodities, goods, and other items that can be measured by wealth.

The political values are centered around power that gives an individual control over a mass of people in a community or national setting. This power is invested in terms of two structural organizations: authoritarianism and democracy.

The religious values recognize the rights and duties of man to worship a Supreme Being. They are based on Christianity and emphasize faith and hope for a better world to come.

The social values are expressed in man's striving to secure basic necessities for survival with a minimum expenditure of energy. They are governed by two trends: (1) stability and security, and (2) adventure, exploration of the unknown, and creation.

The theoretical values aid in one's understanding of himself and other human beings. They provide one with the ability to explore and expedite knowledge for the advancement of himself and his society.

# CHAPTER IV

## METHODOLOGY, COLLECTION, AND TREATMENT OF DATA

### METHODOLOGY

Data was sought from four different classes of students. These students
were college sophomores who were enrolled in a one semester course in educational
psychology class at Mississippi Valley State College, Itta Bena, Mississippi. The
Otis Self-Administering Test of Mental Ability, a standardized group test of intelligence, was used to test one hundred students.

The grade point average was recorded for each student enrolled in the
classes. This average was calculated from tests and examinations given in the
classes, based upon letter grades. Responses from one hundred students were received.

The participants in this study were given an intelligence test to measure
their potential abilities. They were given five assignments which culminated into a
final semester grade, accompanied by grade point averages; they were required to
write a two page essay specifying the value that each held in esteem.

### Collection of Data

The Otis Self-Administering Test, Form A, was administered to four groups
of students enrolled in Education 302 - Educational Psychology at Mississippi Valley
State College during the Fall and Spring Semesters, 1971 and 1972. The test was distributed to the enrolled students and the results were tabulated and compiled by the
researcher.

The criteria for each student receiving a letter grade (A, B, C, D) was
based upon four types of evaluation: (1) mid-semester examination, (2) notebook, (3)
assignments, based upon supplementary materials that came from the library and other
sources of information, and (4) final examination. The letter grade that students
received were translated into grade point averages with A = 4.00, B = 3.00, C = 2.00,
D = 1.00. The grade point average for each student was calculated and recorded for

the class record.

Each participating student was requested to write a two-page essay on the subject, "The Value that I Consider Most Essential." The values were selected from Spranger's Value System, a research on the values held by mankind: namely, theoretical, aesthetic, economic, social, political, religious or philosophical. After the students had written their essays, they were collected and the results compiled by the researcher.

## Treatment of Data

Data on the intelligence quotient and grade point average were translated to IBM unit record cards. Computer programs were prepared to retrieve the necessary data descriptive of the responses from one hundred students. From the computer, data were revealed pertinent to the arithmetic mean, mean deviation, median, and standard deviation for the total number of participating students. The grade point average using the measure of central tendency was computed for ranges assigned to quotients of the students, with I.Q.'s ranging from 80-109.

CHAPTER V

THE RESEARCH RESULTS

<u>INTRODUCTION</u>

This chapter presents a series of tables from Table 1 through Table 10, including a Master Table with assigned numbers, intelligence quotient level, grade point distribution and primary values. It also shows the arithmetic mean, mean deviation, median and standard deviation, taken from the results of the computer program.

This research is based upon the six values held by mankind according to Edward Spranger, the distinguished German Educational Philosopher. These values are: aesthetic, economic, political, religious, social, and theoretical. These values are further divided into two categories: qualitative and quantitative. The qualitative values are those which teachers are most likely to place most emphasis, and the quantitative values are the ones which are likely to be considered secondary or incidental. This research revealed that there is a statistically significant difference in the responses of students who hold in esteem the qualitative values (theoretical, aesthetic and religious) and those who hold in esteem the quantitative values (economic, political, and social).

# TABLE 1

## MASTER TABLE: IDENTIFIED STUDENTS WITH DESIGNATED
## I.Q. LEVELS, GRADE POINT AVERAGES, AND PRIMARY VALUES

| Student Number | I.Q. Level | GPA | Primary Values |
|---|---|---|---|
| 1 | 90- 99 | 2.00 | Religious |
| 2 | 90- 99 | 3.00 | Religious |
| 3 | 80- 89 | 3.00 | Theoretical |
| 4 | 90- 99 | 3.00 | Religious |
| 5 | 80- 89 | 2.00 | Theoretical |
| 6 | 100-109 | 3.00 | Social |
| 7 | 90- 99 | 3.00 | Social |
| 8 | 100-109 | 2.00 | Social |
| 9 | 100-109 | 2.00 | Economic |
| 10 | 100-109 | 1.00 | Theoretical |
| 11 | 90- 99 | 2.00 | Theoretical |
| 12 | 90- 99 | 3.00 | Religious |
| 13 | 80- 89 | 2.00 | Economic |
| 14 | 80- 89 | 3.00 | Theoretical |
| 15 | 90- 99 | 4.00 | Religious |
| 16 | 90- 99 | 2.00 | Political |
| 17 | 90- 99 | 2.00 | Religious |
| 18 | 80- 89 | 2.00 | Religious |
| 19 | 80- 89 | 2.00 | Economic |
| 20 | 80- 89 | 2.00 | Theoretical |
| 21 | 80- 89 | 2.00 | Theoretical |
| 22 | 80- 89 | 2.00 | Theoretical |
| 23 | 90- 99 | 3.00 | Theoretical |

| Student Number | I.Q. Level | GPA | Primary Values |
|---|---|---|---|
| 24 | 100-109 | 2.00 | Religious |
| 25 | 90- 99 | 2.00 | Economic |
| 26 | 80- 89 | 3.00 | Aesthetic |
| 27 | 90- 99 | 3.00 | Social |
| 28 | 100-109 | 3.00 | Social |
| 29 | 100-109 | 3.00 | Political |
| 30 | 80- 89 | 3.00 | Social |
| 31 | 90- 99 | 3.00 | Economic |
| 32 | 90- 99 | 3.00 | Religious |
| 33 | 80- 89 | 4.00 | Religious |
| 34 | 100-109 | 3.00 | Theoretical |
| 35 | 80- 89 | 2.00 | Theoretical |
| 36 | 90- 99 | 2.00 | Social |
| 37 | 100-109 | 2.00 | Religious |
| 38 | 80- 89 | 2.00 | Theoretical |
| 39 | 80- 89 | 2.00 | Social |
| 40 | 80- 89 | 1.00 | Religious |
| 41 | 80- 89 | 2.00 | Social |
| 42 | 90- 99 | 2.00 | Social |
| 43 | 90- 99 | 3.00 | Social |
| 44 | 80- 89 | 3.00 | Social |
| 45 | 100-109 | 3.00 | Political |
| 46 | 90- 99 | 3.00 | Theoretical |
| 47 | 90- 99 | 3.00 | Political |
| 48 | 90- 99 | 3.00 | Theoretical |

| Student Number | I.Q. Level | GPA | Primary Values |
|---|---|---|---|
| 49 | 90- 99 | 4.00 | Religious |
| 50 | 90- 99 | 2.00 | Religious |
| 51 | 80- 89 | 2.00 | Economic |
| 52 | 80- 89 | 3.00 | Economic |
| 53 | 80- 89 | 2.00 | Religious |
| 54 | 90- 99 | 4.00 | Social |
| 55 | 90- 99 | 2.00 | Religious |
| 56 | 80- 89 | 2.00 | Theoretical |
| 57 | 90- 99 | 3.00 | Theoretical |
| 58 | 80- 89 | 2.00 | Economic |
| 59 | 80- 89 | 2.00 | Theoretical |
| 60 | 80- 89 | 2.00 | Religious |
| 61 | 80- 89 | 2.00 | Theoretical |
| 62 | 90- 99 | 3.00 | Religious |
| 63 | 80- 89 | 2.00 | Social |
| 64 | 90- 99 | 2.00 | Religious |
| 65 | 80- 89 | 2.00 | Social |
| 66 | 90- 99 | 3.00 | Theoretical |
| 67 | 80- 89 | 3.00 | Social |
| 68 | 90- 99 | 4.00 | Aesthetic |
| 69 | 90- 99 | 2.00 | Economic |
| 70 | 90- 99 | 2.00 | Economic |
| 71 | 80- 89 | 3.00 | Social |
| 72 | 90- 99 | 2.00 | Religious |
| 73 | 80- 89 | 1.00 | Theoretical |

| Student Number | I.Q. Level | GPA | Primary Values |
|---|---|---|---|
| 74 | 90- 99 | 2.00 | Theoretical |
| 75 | 80- 89 | 1.00 | Theoretical |
| 76 | 80- 89 | 2.00 | Economic |
| 77 | 100-109 | 2.00 | Theoretical |
| 78 | 90- 99 | 2.00 | Economic |
| 79 | 80- 89 | 3.00 | Economic |
| 80 | 90- 99 | 3.00 | Religious |
| 81 | 90- 99 | 2.00 | Religious |
| 82 | 80- 89 | 3.00 | Social |
| 83 | 80- 89 | 1.00 | Religious |
| 84 | 100-109 | 2.00 | Social |
| 85 | 80- 89 | 2.00 | Social |
| 86 | 80- 89 | 3.00 | Economic |
| 87 | 90- 99 | 2.00 | Theoretical |
| 88 | 100-109 | 3.00 | Theoretical |
| 89 | 100-109 | 3.00 | Aesthetic |
| 90 | 90- 99 | 2.00 | Economic |
| 91 | 90- 99 | 2.00 | Social |
| 92 | 80- 89 | 2.00 | Religious |
| 93 | 80- 89 | 3.00 | Theoretical |
| 94 | 80- 89 | 2.00 | Religious |
| 95 | 90- 99 | 3.00 | Social |
| 96 | 80- 89 | 3.00 | Theoretical |
| 97 | 80- 89 | 3.00 | Social |
| 98 | 90- 99 | 3.00 | Social |

| Student Number | I.Q. Level | GPA | Primary Values |
|---|---|---|---|
| 99 | 80- 89 | 2.00 | Social |
| 100 | 80- 89 | 3.00 | Theoretical |

TABLE 2

DISTRIBUTION OF STUDENT POPULATION BY I.Q. LEVELS

| I.Q. Level | Percent |
|---|---|
| 100-109 | 14.0 |
| 90- 99 | 41.0 |
| 80- 89 | 45.0 |
| TOTAL | 100.0 |

Table 2 shows that 14 percent of the participating students in the study scored 100-109 level of intelligence quotient; 41 per cent scored 90-99 level of intelligence quotient and 45 percent scored 80-89 level of intelligence quotient. The mean of I.Q. level is 1.69. The mean of percentage is 33.33.

TABLE 3

DISTRIBUTION OF STUDENT POPULATION BY GRADE POINT AVERAGES

| GPA | Percent |
|---|---|
| 4.00 | 5.0 |
| 3.00 | 39.0 |
| 2.00 | 51.0 |
| 1.00 | 5.0 |
| TOTAL | 100.0 |

Table 3 reveals that 5 percent of the students had a grade point average of 4.00 (A); 39 percent had a grade point average of 3.00 (B); 51 percent had a grade point average of 2.00 (C); and 5 percent had a grade point average of 1.00. The mean of the GPA is 2.44. The mean of percentage is 25.00

TABLE 4

DISTRIBUTION BY STUDENT POPULATION OF PRIMARY VALUES HELD

| Primary Values | Percent |
|---|---|
| Theoretical | 27.0 |
| Religious | 25.0 |
| Social | 25.0 |
| Economic | 16.0 |
| Political | 4.0 |
| Aesthetic | 3.0 |
| TOTAL | 100.0 |

TABLE 5

DISTRIBUTION OF STUDENT POPULATION BY QUALITATIVE VALUES HELD

| Qualitative Values | Percent |
|---|---|
| Theoretical | 27.0 |
| Religious | 25.0 |
| Aesthetic | 3.0 |
| TOTAL | 55.0 |

Table 5 discloses that 55 percent of the students claimed the qualitative values. Of this number, 27 percent listed the theoretical value; 25 percent listed the religious value, and 3 percent listed the aesthetic value.

TABLE 6

DISTRIBUTION OF STUDENT POPULATION BY QUANTITATIVE VALUES HELD

| Quantitative Values | Percent |
|---|---|
| Economic | 16.0 |
| Social | 25.0 |
| Political | 4.0 |
| TOTAL | 45.0 |

Table 6 exemplifies that 45 percent of the students adhered to the quantitative values. Of this number, 16 percent listed the economic values; 25 percent listed the social value, and 4 percent listed the political value.

41

# TABLE 7

DISTRIBUTION OF STUDENT POPULATION HOLDING PRIMARY VALUES
BY GRADE POINT AVERAGE EARNED

| Primary | GPA 4.00 N=5 | GPA 3.00 N=38 | GPA 2.00 N=51 | GPA 1.00 N=5 |
|---------|------|------|------|------|
| Aesthetic | 20 | 5.0 | - | - |
| Economic | - | 10.0 | 22 | 20 |
| Political | - | 7.5 | 2 | - |
| Religious | 60 | 17.5 | 27 | 20 |
| Social | 20 | 32.5 | 22 | - |
| Theoretical | - | 27.5 | 27 | 60 |
| TOTAL | 100 | 100 | 100 | 100 |

Table 7 illustrates the selection patterns of the primary values by students with varying grade point averages: (A) 4.00, (B) 3.00, (C) 2.00, and (D) 1.00. Of the total number who made a grade of A, 20 percent listed the aesthetic value, 60 percent listed the religious value, and 20 percent listed the social value. Of the total number who made a grade of B, 5 percent listed the aesthetic value, 10 percent listed the economic value, 7.5 percent listed the political value, 17.5 listed the religious value, 32.5 percent listed the social value and 27.5 percent listed the theoretical value. Of the total number who made a grade of C, none listed the aesthetic value, 22 percent listed the economic value, 2 percent listed the political value, 27 percent listed the religious value, 22 percent listed the social value, and 27 percent listed the theoretical value. Of the total number who made a grade of D, none listed the aesthetic, political or social values. Twenty percent listed the economic value, 20 percent listed the religious value, and 60 percent listed the theoretical value.

TABLE 8

DISTRIBUTION OF STUDENT POPULATION HOLDING PRIMARY VALUES
BY LEVEL OF INTELLIGENCE QUOTIENT

| Primary Values | 100-109 I.Q. Level N=14 | 90-99 I.Q. Level N=41 | 80-89 I.Q. Level N=45 |
|---|---|---|---|
| Aesthetic | 7 | 2 | 2 |
| Economic | 7 | 14 | 20 |
| Political | 14 | 5 | - |
| Religious | 14 | 38 | 18 |
| Social | 29 | 22 | 27 |
| Theoretical | 29 | 19 | 33 |
| TOTAL | 100 | 100 | 100 |

Table 8 displays the distribution of student population holding primary values with intelligence quotient levels. Students with 100-109 I.Q. levels listed aesthetic 7 percent, economic 7 percent, political 14 percent, religious 14 percent, social 29 percent, and theoretical 29 percent. Students with 90-99 I.Q. levels listed aesthetic 2 percent, economic 14 percent, political 5 percent, religious 38 percent, social 22 percent, and theoretical 19 percent. Students with 80-89 I.Q. levels listed aesthetic 2 percent, economic 20 percent, religious 18 percent, social 27 percent, and theoretical 33 percent.

TABLE 9

DISTRIBUTION OF STUDENT POPULATION
BY GRADE POINT AVERAGES AND I.Q. LEVELS

| I.Q. Levels | GPA 4.00 N=5 | GPA 3.00 N=39 | GPA 2.00 N=51 | GPA 1.00 N=5 |
|---|---|---|---|---|
| 100-109 | - | 18.0 | 12.0 | 20.0 |
| 90- 99 | 80.0 | 43.0 | 40.0 | - |
| 80- 89 | 20.0 | 39.0 | 48.0 | 80.0 |
| TOTAL | 100.0 | 100.0 | 100.0 | 100.0 |

Table 9 reveals the selection patterns of grade point averages and I.Q. levels of students with (A) 4.00, (B) 3.00, (C) 2.00, and (D) 1.00. Of the students who made a grade of A, none scored on the 100-109 I.Q. level, 80 percent scored on the 90-99 I.Q. level, and 20 percent scored on the 80-89 I.Q. level. Of the students who made a grade of B, 18 percent scored on the 100-109 I.Q. level, 43 percent scored on the 90-99 I.Q. level, and 39 percent scored on the 80-89 I.Q. level. Of the students who made a grade of (C), 12 percent scored 100-109 I.Q. level, 40 percent scored 90-99 I.Q. level, and 48 percent scored 80-89 I.Q. level. Of the students who made a grade of D, 20 percent scored 100-109 I.Q. level, none scored 90-99 I.Q. level, and 80 percent scored 80-89 I.Q. level.

## TABLE 10

COMPUTER RESULTS OF ARITHMETIC MEAN, MEAN DEVIATION, MEDIAN
AND STANDARD DEVIATION OF THE TOTAL NUMBER OF STUDENTS WITH
HIGH, MEDIUM, AND LOW I.Q.'S

| Grade Point Average | Total Number Students | 100-109 I.Q. | 90-99 I.Q. | 80-89 I.Q. |
|---|---|---|---|---|
| Arithmetic Mean | 25.00 | 3.50 | 9.75 | 11.75 |
| Mean Deviation | 20.00 | 3.00 | 7.75 | 9.25 |
| Median | 22.00 | 3.50 | 10.00 | 10.00 |
| Standard Deviation | 20.44 | 3.04 | 7.94 | 9.96 |

Of particular significance, the computer analyses revealed the results of the Arithmetic Mean, Mean Deviation, Median, and Standard Deviation and intelligence level of students. For 100-109 I.Q. students the Arithmetic Mean was 3.50, Mean Deviation 3.00, Median 3.50 and Standard Deviation 3.04. For 90-99 I.Q. students the Arithmetic Mean was 9.75, Mean Deviation 7.75, Median 10.00 and Standard Deviation 7.94. For 80-89 I.Q. students the Arithmetic Mean was 11.75, Mean Deviation 9.25, Median 10.00, and Standard Deviation 9.96.

# CHAPTER VI

## STUDENT INTERPRETATIONS OF ESTEEM VALUES

### INTRODUCTION

This portion of the research dealing with students interpretations of esteem values: aesthetic, economic, political, religious, social, and theoretical, is divided into two sections. The first part consists of major statements on each of the esteem values, taken from the students' essays. These statements were compiled in order to reveal the significance the students attached to these values. The second part consists of a representative number of essays on each of the esteem values that were written by the students.

### Aesthetic Value

1. Aesthetics reveals the beautiful things of life.

2. Aesthetics is the work of arts and reveals the beauty of the common place.

3. Aesthetics provides the basis for an appreciation of our cultural heritage.

### Economic Value

1. Economic value prevents the world from being poverty stricken.

2. Economizing is a way to progress and a better way of life.

3. Economic value reveals to man the nature and distribution of goods.

4. Economics teaches the concept of thrift and efficiency.

5. Economics teaches one to budget his income for present and future usage.

### Political Value

1. Political value is the key to first-class citizenship.

2. Political value is essential in exercising one's privilege to vote.

3. Political value gives power in promoting and gaining freedom.

## Religious Value

1. Religion is faith in God that continues throughout one's lifetime.

2. Religion means putting God into our lives.

3. Religion requires "faith" something few people possess.

4. Religion enables one to cling to a higher power than man.

5. Religious ideas should be taught as a base for moral and spiritual values.

6. Religious value fosters every ingredient for a wholesome and abundant life.

7. Religion influences justice and fair play in one's dealing.

8. Religion is most valuable because it includes a code of ethics and conduct.

## Social Value

1. Social value is concerned with the welfare of others.

2. Friends and humans contact are by-products of social relationships.

3. Social value provides security in fulfilling our personal needs.

4. Social value provides a sense of belonging to a group.

## Theoretical Value

1. Knowledge is the product of knowing, informing, or understanding.

2. Knowledge is a prerequisite to thinking and planning.

3. Knowledge is one of the most precious things in life.

4. Knowledge is something that everybody needs.

# CHAPTER VII

## SUMMARY, CONCLUSIONS, AND RECOMMENDATIONS

### INTRODUCTION

There are many problems that beset us in our modern society. Many of these problems stem from our youth in high schools and colleges. Yet, very few teachers think in terms of the underlying motives, concepts or values that they hold are closely allied with their behavioral patterns. It is at this point of origin where this problem probes into the nature of the situation and the availability of the research tools and subjects, the participating students.

This study was limited to one hundred students enrolled in educational psychology classes at Mississippi Valley State College, during the school term 1971-72.

The instruments used for conducting this study were: The Otis Self-Administering Test of Mental Ability; the accumulative grade point averages based upon the mid-semester examination, notebooks, assignments, and the final examination. Students were also requested to write a two-page essay on the priority values that they held in esteem.

### Statement of the Problem

This problem was designed to ascertain the relationship of esteem values held by one hundred college students of educational psychology, their intelligence quotients and grade point averages. Selected esteem values are: aesthetic, economic, political, religious, social and theoretical.

### Purpose of the Study

Research revealed that the Henmon Nelson Test of Mental Ability was an important criterion in assessing students' abilities to succeed in academic performance.

The essential ingredients for continued growth in intelligence are open-mindedness to new ideas and willingness to criticize one's most cherished convictions.

The total grade point average seemed to be the best criterion used for admission to teacher education.

Perhaps the best way to transmit values is to create an atmosphere on campus. Arsenian used the Study of Values to study changes in attitudes during four years of college. He noted some statistically significant changes over the four year period, especially on emphasis placed on religious beliefs.[66]

Every teacher must be prepared to cope with behavior indicative of some inadequacy in value orientation. Without regard to its fuller meaning, the effect on the student's value of orientation may well result in the reinforcement of less mature behavior forms.

## A Synopsis of the Findings

The findings in this research are closely related to the information revealed in the survey of the related literature.

The average student in this study made a grade point average of 2.00 (C). This conforms to the normal probability curve.

The majority of the students who made the lowest grades also had the lowest intelligence quotient.

Research also revealed that for many persons the attainment of intellectual ingredients do not change markedly over a period of time.

This study further revealed that many students hold priority values that are not normally transmitted in the classroom.

## Summary

This study was conducted because there is an element in students' learning that is associated with the values that they hold in esteem.

The values that they held in esteem were based on Spranger's Value System: aesthetic, economic, political, religious, social, and theoretical.

Research revealed that the Henmon Nelson Test of Mental Ability was an important criterion in assessing students' abilities to succeed in academic performance.

Research revealed that the Henmon Nelson Test of Mental Ability was an important criterion in assessing students' abilities to succeed in academic performance.

Publishers of the Otis Test stated that it is a valid measure of general mental ability. It enables a teacher or administrator to measure the native ability of students in groups, to ascertain their native abilities to succeed in academic performance.

Publishers of the Otis Test stated that it is a valid measure of general ability. It enables a teacher or administrator to measure the native ability of students in groups, to ascertain their native capacities to learn, and for guidance purposes.

In a research by William J. Brady, it was stated that the total grade point averages seems to be the best criterion used at the time of admission to teacher education.

Research also reveals that each individual comes to attach significant meanings to certain experience, to value certain experience, and to avoid or reject others.

Patricia S. Plant stated that undergraduate education is intimately related to values which students are attempting to form, and the issues which they must confront are perennial issues of morals, politics, and aesthetics.

The aesthetic value, a synonym for beauty, esteems the work of artists and provides a basis for the appreciation of our cultural heritage.

The economic value reveals to man the nature and distribution of consumer goods.

The political value holds the key to politics and power as a means of exercising one's rights and privilege to vote his conviction in a democratic society.

The religious value fosters the concept of the redemption of man by a power higher than himself, a Supreme Being.

The social value advocates friendly human contact and relationship with other human beings.

The theoretical value esteems knowledge as a process of knowing, with pre-existing knowledge and experience forming the basis for attainment.

# Conclusions

The findings in this research are closely related to the information revealed in the survey of the literature.

1. The average student in this study made a grade point average of 2.00 (C).

2. The majority of students who made the lowest grades also had the lowest intelligence quotients.

3. The research also revealed that for many students the attainments of intellectual ingredients do not change markedly over a period of time.

4. This study further revealed that many students hold priority values that are not normally transmitted in the classroom.

5. Hypothesis 1 stated that there is no relationship between I.Q. scores and qualitative values.

6. Hypothesis 2 stated that there is no relationship between I.Q. scores and quantitative values.

7. Hypothesis 3 stated that there is no relationship between I.Q. scores and aesthetic values.

8. Hypothesis 4 stated that there is no relationship between I.Q. scores and economic values.

Using the coefficient of correlation: $r = 0.336$, which implies from the table that there is no relationship between the aesthetic and economics values as far as the I.Q. is concerned. Therefore, the null hypothesis is accepted for hypothesis 3 and hypothesis 4.

9. Hypothesis 5 stated that there is no relationship between I.Q. scores and political values.

10. Hypothesis 6 stated that there is no relationship between I.Q. scores and religious values.

The coefficient of correlation of $r = 0.992$ implies that there is no relationship between the political and religious values as far as I.Q. is concerned. Therefore, the null hypothesis is accepted for hypothesis 5 and hypothesis 6.

11. Hypothesis 7 stated that there is no relationship between I.Q. scores and social values.

12. Hypothesis 8 stated that there is no relationship between I.Q. scores and theoretical values.

The coefficient of correlation of $\gamma$ = 0.846 implies that there is no relationship between the social and theoretical values as far as I.Q. is concerned, therefore, the null hypothesis is accepted for hypothesis 7 and hypothesis 8.

13. In calculating the coefficient of correlation between the I.Q. of 80-89 versus an I.Q. 90-99, $\gamma$ = 0.986 implies that there is no relationship between an I.Q. 80-89 and I.Q. 90-99 in GPA for students in this study.

14. In calculating the coefficient of correlation between an I.Q. 90-99 versus an I.Q. 100-109, $\gamma$ = 8.888 implies that there is no relationship between an I.Q. 90-99 and I.Q. 100-109 in GPA for students in this study.

15. In calculating the coefficient of correlation between an I.Q. of 80-89 versus an I.Q. 100-109, $\gamma$ = +0.799 implies that there is no relationship between an I.Q. 80-89 and I.Q. 100-109 in GPA for students in this study.

The data taken in reference to the grade point averages and the intelligence quotients of students with reference to <u>arithmetic mean, mean deviation, median, and standard deviation</u> revealed no diagnostics. This means that the information is correct.

16. In the final analysis, this research reveals that:

    a. A great portion of values that students hold are not necessarily related to knowledge gathering techniques, especially those applied to the classroom.

    b. A majority of students who received low grades also had intelligence quotients ranging from 80-89.

    c. Students who made the highest grades were not those who possessed intelligence quotients, ranging from 100-109.

    d. Students who made grades of 3.00 had intelligence quotients ranging from 100-109.

e.  Of the total number of students who made a grade of A, 60 percent listed the religious value.

f.  Of the total number of students who made a grade of C, none listed the aesthetic value.

g.  Thirty-three percent of students with I.Q.'s 80-89 listed the theoretical value as their priority value.

h.  The average grade point of 2.00 made by the majority of students was reported in research studies in 80 percent of the institutions as adequate for admission to a program leading to certification.

i.  There is a statistically significant difference in the responses of students who hold in esteem the qualitative values (theoretical, aesthetic, religious) and those who hold in esteem the quantitative values (social, economic, political).

j.  Students who had continuity experiences in value identification were better able to meet the problems of daily life than those who lack such experiences, and that the social studies offer an effective vehicle for value classification.

k.  Teachers who participated in small discussion groups that enabled the student to express themselves about the problems that they were facing in the classroom gained a better perspective in relating positively to their students than non-participating teachers.

l.  The basic information gained from this study can be applied by teachers and research workers who are concerned with training and education of students.

## Recommendations for Development

It is recommended that this study be undertaken on a larger scale, including a greater number of participants, in order to validate or refute the claims made in this study.

It is further recommended that a follow-up be initiated after the students have finished the four-year course to ascertain whether values selected are constant and flexible.

## Recommendations for Further Study

It is recommended that:

1.  A similar study be conducted with a high school group to denote the

relationship of primary values held by students at the high school level with those at the college level.

2. Experimental studies on student values be conducted because they reflect current thinking of students which is not necessarily in keeping with students' thinking a generation ago.

3. Research workers assist teachers and others interested in the learning process of the significance found in student value orientation.

# APPENDIX

## WHY I CONSIDER THE <u>ECONOMIC</u> VALUE MOST IMPORTANT

By
Student A

Well, the main reason I consider the economic value most important is because it is the study of the social organization by means of which people of a society satisfy their wants for scarce goods and services. It is not primarily concerned with the activities of individuals, but rather with their relations to one another and with the social institutions they have created to facilitate the production, distribution, and consumption of goods. Because earning a living is a very urgent and time consuming activity in all human societies, economic consideration permeates the whole of human life and have had an incalculably great influence in shaping human cultures and human societies.

Economic wants are desires for things that can be obtained by labor or though exchange, and upon which, in a modern society, a money value can be placed. This is necessarily so, because if any group is to survive, it must have certain kinds of goods that are relatively scarce and difficult to obtain; and to produce or otherwise acquire such goods necessitates economic activities of the type we usually call labor.

The most universal economic want of human beings, one that cannot be denied, is that for food; even since man first appeared upon the earth, it is pretty certain that most people have spent the greater part of only in modern industrial countries has food become relatively plentiful and easy to obtain.

# WHY I CONSIDER AESTHETIC VALUE MOST IMPORTANT

By
Student B

I consider the aesthetic value most important above all the other values because it defines the beautiful things of life, the loveliness and the joy that a person gets when he experiences such a thing of beauty.

Aesthetic is important because it also conforms the social life of a person which tells of the art of beauty which is encountered in his environment, which all goes back to the beautiful happenings that occurred in the past as well as the present. For example: the joy and happiness that you remember when you found your first girl friend or your first boy friend, going to a very popular concert, or even a movie. It's the beautiful things that derive from being aesthetic, always looking for the lovely, beautiful and joyful things that life and happiness can only bring.

Aesthetic doesn't mean that this beauty or loveliness can't be imparted upon by sorrow or hatred or even grief because it can and will if you are one who will let it happen. But let us say that at times some things just can't be helped, but life must go on regardless of the mishaps; some rain must fall in every one's life at some time. This is why I feel that the value of aesthetic is most important over all the other values.

# WHY I CONSIDER THE THEORETICAL VALUE MOST IMPORTANT

By
Student C

The reason I consider the theoretical value most important is because I think knowledge is the most precious thing in life. Knowledge is the product of knowing, informing, or understanding acquired through experience, practical ability, or skill, and life depends on these things.

If a person doesn't know anything it will be hard for him to go through life easily as a person that knows something. For example when a person goes to look for a job, the first questions asked are: What do you know, do you have any type of experience?

Knowledge is connected in the most definite manner with the life of the spirit of man, such a spiritual life has to discover itself within the movement of universal history and to unfold itself more and more within this movement, so that it becomes indispensable for thought to grasp and to preserve such a situation. Our spiritual life also depends upon knowledge.

In order to do something in life and do it well we must have some type of knowledge of how it must be done.

Knowledge is the key to understanding. In order to be successful in life you must understand. Understanding that is knowledge makes life easy.

If a man didn't have any type of knowledge of how to build a house, we wouldn't have a place to stay. Since man has some type of knowledge, we have a nice place to live, airplanes and cars to ride in. Therefore, I conclude that knowledge is one of the most precious things in life.

# WHY I CONSIDER RELIGIOUS VALUES MOST IMPORTANT

By
Student D

I consider religious values most important because without it a person never knows the true meaning of love and security. Religious values are a condition of life that will be  with us as long as we live. When we are children, our parents and teachers guide our conduct and establish our pattern for growing up in the right way.

As the years pass, however, each of us realizes more and more that the true faith must come from within. To be successful in college, we must have faith in God to help us develop good study habits and stay with them. Not only do we need God in school, but in our everyday walk of life. With God all things are possible.

An intelligent man looks for religious activities. He sees and does things, he goes places, and he learns by seeing, doing, and going. He figures that life provides things and ideas to be sampled, understood, and appreciated for his own benefit.

For the religious man there are those awarding moments in his life that are meant for peace and quiet thinking. If his faith is to be at all meaningful to him, it must be given meaning by putting it into his existence.

Religious for living in a changing age should mean more for us than merely taking out time to go to church on Sunday. We should not put God aside until we need him. We should appreciate also the effects it might have on man and on the world in which he lives.

Faith must do more than inspect man, it should train him to do that which is right. It should educate him to love as well as make a living in an increasingly complex and perplexing world. Therefore, I conclude that religious value is most important.

# WHY I CONSIDER THE ECONOMIC VALUE MOST IMPORTANT

By
Student E

I believe that economics is most important in the world today. If it were not for economics, the world would be poverty-stricken. Many people of the United States have economic budgets. This is where they limit the amount of money spent on such things as food, clothes, household goods, etc.

The economic budget values money problems. The United States has an economic budget so that we as citizens won't go broke. Economizing is the way of progress and a better way of life. I believe the economic system is the best thing that man has ever produced. Since some men have things other men need, if one can not afford it, then he economizes his budget in order that he may secure it at a later date.

Economics goes back almost to the beginning of man, where he used the barter system as well as conserve such items that he had in his possession. In 1950, there were over 100,000 families in the United States who were poverty stricken for not having an economic budget.

In conclusion, I think the economic value is most important because: (a) it reveals to man the nature and distribution of consumer goods, (b) it teaches the concepts of thrift and efficiency in the use of consumer products, and (c) it teaches one how to budget his income for present and future usage.

# WHY I CONSIDER THE <u>RELIGIOUS</u> OR PHILOSOPHICAL VALUE

By
Student F

There are many reasons for my belief of, "Religion or the Philosophical Value of Life." Although I think other values are important, I do think religion should be the most important in the life of an individual.

Religion requires "faith" something few people possess; philosophical value or the philosophy - principles and ethics, which few people can accept. An individual life should be a goal built on faith, principles, ethics and a pattern. A pattern either formed by one's self but with the help and knowledge of someone else that is higher not only in stature but in supremacy - God.

To believe that man does not sustain himself but answers to a higher authority can easily be accepted when a person looks at the conditions of the world. Look around (not necessarily the world) but your own community and see the problems of poverty for some people and wealth for others, envy and jealousy of families and friends alike; to look at the corruptions and ills of man should be a search for something more reliable and more stable which can be found in religion.

If a person is seeking everlasting peace and tranquility, then religion or some philosophical values must be attained and believed.

60

# WHY I CONSIDER THE SOCIAL VALUE MOST IMPORTANT

By
Student G

I chose to write on Edward Spranger's social value which states that the social is one who holds friendly human contacts relatively higher than other goods.

I think this theory is the most important because it is concerned with the essential quality of man. I also think that friendship and the concern for the welfare of others should be considered an essential product for the survival of mankind.

You can imagine what today's society would be like if everyone would think of himself only. What would happen to all of the poor people who depend on help from others for mere existence? What would happen to all of the people in the undeveloped countries of the Far East, who depend upon the aid from people in other countries to help carry on their survival?

Living a life without friends would be a terrible way to live. If you have a problem all you have to do is to go to that friend for a solution or answer to the problem. People just feel much better when they have someone they can trust. Usually one feels much better when he can talk his problem over with someone. If a friend will tell you what he thinks is best, you can easily make your decision. Really, the social value is just as important as money to me.

# WHY I CONSIDER THE <u>SOCIAL</u> VALUE MOST IMPORTANT

By
Student H

The reason that I consider the social value most important is because the moral standard of the child is influenced by the special group to which the family belongs. Different social groups and different moral standards have their impact upon the child during infancy and early childhood. The family's economic condition will affect the size the house and the amount of play space available. Children from middle class homes are likely to be closely supervised in their education and future than those from the lower class homes. The lower cultural level parents regard certain types of behavior inherently rather than harmful because of the consequences. An important reason why many upper middle class parents don't want their children to go to a certain school is that they don't want their children to talk and behave like children from the lower class or from the slum areas. Scientific studies show ways of which children from different socio-economic status as well as those of different socio-economic groups. It is important for the teacher to understand variations within each group as well as the broad differences among groups. These are the main reasons why I consider the social value to be the most important.

# WHY I CONSIDER THE <u>RELIGIOUS</u> VALUE MOST IMPORTANT

By
Student I

I believe everyone has values that he places on his life. I agree that some values play a part that is more important than others. Of these I hold that the religious value is of greatest significance.

Since religion in itself tends to hold a degree of mysticism for man, it keeps man ever involved in an attempt to justify his action through the scales of morality. This leads me to say that our society is usually formed in connection with a local church, which determines its activities.

When scientific explanations of life's problems and mysteries have proved inadequate, when tensions seem unbearable, peace may be attained through faith in the ultimate wisdom of a Supreme Being.

I think that religious ideas give a solid foundation to the democratic values. Religious ideas should be taught as a base for moral and spiritual values. This teaching can help to decrease crime and juvenile delinquency, and cause a new interest in the basic values of our culture.

In speaking of religious values or religion, I am in a position to speak most favorably about christianity. I speak of it as a "motivating tool." This religion has sought to establish a workable system of practical morality. Every ingredient for a wholesome and abundant living may be found in the religious values proposed by christianity.

The greater bulk of justice, fair-play and even mercy have persuaded most of civilization today, because of the influence of religious values. One can see that values are as empty rhetoric, simply implies "special standards," designed for special interest. On the other hand, values as communal goals reach for cooperative and interdependent relationships with one's fellowman.

Therefore, I feel that the most powerful single influence in all history has been religion and the values set by it. This may not only be noted in the

63

religious beliefs and spiritual ideals of the human race, but in the march of political events and institutions as well.  The unwavering strength of our society hinges itself on the belief in religious values, however, little or much they are lived.

# WHY I CONSIDER THE <u>SOCIAL</u> VALUE MOST IMPORTANT

By
Student J

I feel that social contact is the most important factor in a person's life because all the money in the world won't buy happiness, love, and that wonderful feeling of being needed.

When I say happiness I mean the feeling of belonging to a group. Everyone needs friends if its only for protection because there are so many groups of young men and women going around taking advantage of others. Being in a group can also mean that you can do certain things that you could not do alone. Such things as playing ball, singing certain songs and playing cards.

Not only belonging to a group is considered important, but having that one main friend, that you can tell your troubles to. That friend you consider your personal friend, your love one, plays an important role, in your life also, because he's that person in which you feel secure with.

Another reason why I consider social contact most important is that wonderful feeling of being needed. Although a few people will walk around saying they don't need anyone for anything, they are only fooling themselves or trying to put themselves over everyone else for the feeling of honor or the feeling of being different from everyone else. I feel that every person or animal needs at least one friend and that secure feeling of walking around in a friendly neighborhood helping someone in some way, if it was only making someone feel your presence. The greatest feeling is hearing them say they need you and mean it. I'm not talking about a person that tries to use another but a person that needs another person to talk to or to share his problems with.

These are only a few reasons why I consider social value to be the most important.

# WHY I FEEL THAT THE THEORETICAL VALUE MOST IMPORTANT

By
Student L

I feel that knowledge is the essence of a worthy life. You've got to have knowledge in order to be the man that will make success in life. I feel to this theory that knowledge comes from a great degree of (C.S.), Common Sense. Using your brain for something more than a hat rack. A person who has (C.S.) can very well be a man who has mastered all six of the main values of life given by the German Educational Philosopher, Edward Spranger. They are:

1. Theoretical
2. Aesthetic
3. Economic
4. Social
5. Political
6. Philosophical

In today's time you have to be very educated in order to understand fine arts, or be able to understand the beauty of sculptor. One might make the mistake of selling a million dollars painting for ten dollars or something less than that.

One can hardly save today unless he has some kind of knowledge toward things of economical value. We are living an inflationary period and in order to save when you go to the store, you have to have plenty of sense. If a person is not economically inclined and able to budget his money, he will be caught with a big bill at the end of the month, with no money in the bank, and not able to borrow any.

It is very bad when a person does not know how to treat another human being. A person with good social, friendly, and common sense, contact with others know how to treat people. It is good to learn early in life that the people you meet going up you will meet them coming down. If you had just a little time to think, you would see what I mean.

Many people try for political offices and most of them don't even know what the office that they are seeking for really means. The man that I vote for must have some knowledge of what the people need. He may have the qualification,

66

but his interest for his people is lacking.  Therefore, when I vote a man in I will feel completely convinced in him as being the man with plenty of (C.S.).

For the most part all human beings have some kind of religion.  A man without a religion is like a man without a name.  Man believes in his religion by what knowledge he has of it.  People who are true to their faith read to learn more about it and when they read knowledge is acquired.  When a person has knowledge of his religion, he is able to spread it all over the land.

Therefore, in my conclusion knowledge is mandatory to master any of the six values of life stated by Dr. Spranger.  Knowledge is something that all men strive for because without it you are nothing.

# WHY I CONSIDER THE ECONOMIC VALUE IMPORTANT

By
Student M

The qualitative problem is how the different kinds of goods shall be allocated among the different individuals. The quantitative problem in distribution is how much shall go to each individual. Certain assumptions have to be made about human satisfaction or welfare, including the principle of diminishing marginal substituitability between goods. The prices of the goods can be made to reflect their circumstances of which the government may interfere with the optimum allocation of goods.

The acquisition through experience of capacity to enjoy income, an unequal diversion would be the optimum, but concessions that have to be made for other reasons meet this point too. To reject the conclusion that the optimum division is an equal one is not more impartial or scientific than to accept the assumption on which it is based.

Money income can be used to represent real income even if prices change. To obtain criteria for the optimum division of money income we must assume that different people enjoy similar satisfactions and that the principle of diminishing marginal utility of income holds generally.

In conclusion, based on the finding in the review of related literature it was shown that Economic Value helps in many ways. Some ways are: (a) the price of goods, (b) the individual learns how to manage his business, (c) one knows where his income is going. There are just a few ways that I think Economic Value is important.

# WHY I CONSIDER <u>RELIGIOUS</u> VALUE MOST IMPORTANT

By
Student N

In my opinion religion is the most valuable of Spranger's six main value types. Through religion, man attempts to achieve the highest possible good by adjusting his life to the strongest and best power in the universe. This power that I refer to is called God. I think of God as a good and just individual in whom all things are made possible. I think that my life and destiny depend on forces in the world more powerful than myself.

Without Christ to lean on - life for me would be pointless and definitely endless, especially when I consider the terrible things people have done and said to me. Surely, there has to be a better life after death. I agree with many others who say that one day Christ will separate the good from the bad. Certainly, I hope to be standing on his right side which will consist of the righteous.

Religion is most valuable to me because it includes a code of ethics and conduct. Ethics asks "How should we behave toward other people?" Religion asks: "How should we relate ourselves to the greatest power in the universe?" In other words, the christian doctrine teaches God's love for men and stresses the importance of brotherly love.

I believe that every individual has a belief in a supreme being - one that he turns to especially in times of trouble. Therefore I conclude that the religious value is most important.

# WHY I CONSIDER <u>ECONOMIC</u> VALUE MOST IMPORTANT
By
Student O

Economic education to me has advanced in recent years more than any other segment of the social studies. Concepts such as division of labor are introduced in the beginning grades as children compare the production of cookiness or other items on an "assembly line" where each worker does a special job with complete production of the item by individuals. The differences between producers and consumers and goods and services are discovered as children investigate roles of members of the family, community workers, and consume various goods and services.

Economists have been quite active in working with school personnel to plan the social studies curriculum. The result has been a widespread agreement that the following items should be included in social studies instruction.

Conflict exists among wants and resources, scarcity, division of labor, specialization, interdependence, goods, services, consumers, producers, factors of production, or productive resources, production, consumption, exchange, distribution, market, supply, demand, prices, money, banking, credit, savings, spending, investing trade, inputs, outputs, economic systems, economic values, and opportunity cost principle.

Basic Economic Problem - conflict between wants and labor, resources, need to make choices, need for an economic system to allocate resources to alternative uses. These and other reasons are essential in my selecting the economic value as most important.

# WHY I CONSIDER POLITICAL VALUE MOST IMPORTANT

By
Student R

I consider the political value as being most important to me. There are several reasons why the political value is most important. As a black man I feel that the only way to get ahead is through the political system. In order to be a first class citizen you must exercise your privilege to vote. Then and only then will the black man gain the respectability that he has long deserved. The problem that we are facing is due in part by our lack of political socialization, not only in the school, but I think it must start in the home. We must make a change and it must be soon, if our people are ever to live in peace in America. We, as black people, must look upon the political value as being the best and safest way out, because revolution is not the answer; it would only demolish the progress that we, as the people, have made throughout the years. We must not let what our brothers and sisters have gone through to give us political freedom go to waste, some have died, others gone to jail and countless others harrassments. The political value has to be looked at seriously, because black power is dead without political power. As citizens are becoming more urbanized by blacks, I consider this to be a golden opportunity for blacks to enter into the political system; therefore, I consider the political value most important.

# WHY I CONSIDER THE <u>RELIGIOUS</u> OR PHILOSOPHICAL VALUE MOST IMPORTANT

By
Student S

I feel that the religious or philosophical value of one finding his main satisfaction in his relations to the whole of experience is most important of all of Spranger's values in that I feel man cannot know true satisfaction until he has experienced the whole of life and the world. Also man has to have some religious basis before he even knows what satisfaction is. All of man's successes, accomplishments, and satisfactions come first of all from God because without God man would fail and be nothing.

I personally feel that no man can be truly satisfied with just his knowledge or art or his material possessions or his friends or power. I do feel that these things are not real values but, rather goals or desires. A man who places these things the highest among their so-called values really has nothing because he has not experienced everything. If one has some of all of these things then he has values.

This makes up the whole of his experiences. No man should claim his earthly possessions more valuable than the possessions which God is preparing for him. God does allow us to have things here on earth, but these can in no way compare to the heavenly possessions we will one day inherit as a reward for our life here on earth.

A man only has a half-life if he does not experience everything. He has a one-sided system of values mainly because he has experienced a very few things; therefore, he can only place his values on those things which he has experienced. For this reason I feel that until one has experienced the whole, then he does not know what true values are.

# WHY I CONSIDER THE ECONOMIC VALUE MOST IMPORTANT

By
Student T

I believe that economics is most important in the world today. If it were not for economics, the world would be poverty-stricken. Many people of the United States have economic budgets. This is where they limit the amount of money spent on such goods as food, clothes, household goods, etc.

The economic budget values money problems. The United States has an economic budget so that we as citizens won't go broke. Economizing is the way of progress and a better way of life. I believe the economic system is the best thing that man has ever produced. Since some men have things other men need, if one can not afford it, then he economizes his budget in order that he may secure it at a later date.

Economics goes back almost to the beginning of man, where he used the barter system as well as conserve such items that he had in his possession. In 1950, there were over 100,000 families in the United States who were poverty-stricken for not having an economic budget.

In conclusion, I think the economic value is most important because: (a) it reveals to man the nature and distribution of consumer goods, (b) it teaches the concepts of thrift and efficiency in the use of consumer products, and (c) it teaches one how to budget his income for present and future usage.

# WHY I CONSIDER THE <u>THEORETICAL</u> VALUE MOST IMPORTANT

By
Student W

I feel personally that the theoretical value, is most important, because if one has the knowledge, there are many things one can accomplish. Knowledge is most important to me, because in this society in which we live, one has to have some idea about the environment he's surrounded by.

The theoretical value is important along with many other values. The reason for stating this is because I do feel for one to get an understanding, he has to accomplish the goal of knowledge in order to accept the values offered him in many other values, once knowledge is well acquired. I haven't taken values in the many different forms especially individually, as one precious thought of the mind.

The theoretical value, is one that is deep concern, because knowledge is something everyone needs. Knowledge is my main purpose to achieve. I don't think that I could accomplish in life any one thing successfully without some background of what I want or take interest in.

In conclusion, I would like to say the other important values are also of some importance. As stated before, once I have acquired the knowledge I can appreciate the many other values offered me and many others who feel somewhat the same way I feel toward the theoretical value.

# WHY I CONSIDER THE <u>RELIGIOUS</u> VALUE MOST IMPORTANT

By
Student Y

Religion seeks to discover values and to attract men to them through worship and discipline.

In religion we ask ourselves the question:  "How can we relate ourselves to the greatest power in the universe?"  Religion is one of the most powerful forces in history, millions of persons have died for their religious beliefs.  Many nations have gone to war to spread or defend their faiths.

Sooner or later persons come to believe that their lives depend on forces in the universe more powerful than themselves.  They identify these powers, regard them with awe, and seek good relations with them, which becomes their dieties (gods).

Religions teach you that selfishness is evil; love is the goal of human relationships.  It condemns murder, theft, adultery, and dishonesty.  It also teaches us to "treat others as we would have them to treat us."

Another reason why I selected religious value is because I know that God is the Noblest Being in the universe.  Religion places great emphasis on the individual.  One carries out the religious teaching influences all aspects of a person's life.  For example, religious values give the individual a framework for judging right from wrong and for living a good life.

# FOOTNOTES

1. Robin M. Williams, Jr., <u>American Society: A Sociological Interpretation</u> (New York: Knopf Publishing Company, 1960), p. 469.

2. Leonard Broom and Others, <u>Sociology</u> (New York: Harper and Row Publishing Company, 1968), p. 54.

3. Robin M. Williams, Jr., <u>American Society: A Sociological Interpretation</u> (New York: Knopf Publishing Company, 1960), p. 470.

4. Henry Clay Lindgreen, and Others, <u>Psychology: An Introduction to Behavioral Science</u> (New York: John Wiley & Sons, 1966), p. 516.

5. Charles E. Skinner, <u>Elementary Educational Psychology</u> (New York: Prentice-Hall, Inc., 1954), p. 421.

6. <u>Ibid</u>., p. 6.

7. <u>Ibid</u>., p. 424.

8. Anne Anastasti, <u>Psychological Testing</u> (New York: The Macmillan Company, 1941), p. 5.

9. <u>Ibid</u>., p. 6.

10. Lucille Bowie and Morgan Gerthon, "Personal Values and Verbal Behavior," <u>Journal of Experimental Education,</u> XXX (March, 1952), p. 337.

11. Joseph Raymond Johnson, <u>A History of Millersbury Military Institute</u> (Unpublished Doctoral Dissertation, Laurence University, 1971), p. 32.

12. Fillmore H. Sanford, <u>Psychology: A Scientific Study of Man</u> (Belmont, California: Wadsworth Publishing Company, 1967), p. 140.

13. <u>Ibid</u>., p. 141.

14. Oscar K. Buros, <u>The Sixth Mental Measurement Yearbook</u> (Highland Park, New Jersey: The Gryphon Press, 1965), pp. 480-481.

15. Norman L. Munn, <u>Psychology: The Fundamentals of Human Adjustment</u> (Boston: Houghton Mifflin Company, 1966), p. 126.

16. Arthur W. Combs and Donald Syngg, <u>Individual Behavior</u> (New York: Harper & Row, 1959), p. 216.

17. Morris L. Bigge and Maurice P. Hunt, <u>Psychological Foundations of Education</u> (New York: Harper and Row Publishers, 1968), p. 480.

18. William J. Brady, "Twenty Quantitative Predictors of Academic Success as Measured by Grade Point Averages," (Unpublished Doctoral Dissertation, University of Connecticut, 1965), p. 83.

19. Robert E. Hill, Jr., "Scholastic Success of College Freshmen from Parochial and Public Secondary Schools," <u>The School Review</u>, 1961, p. 60.

20. Patricia J. Bond, "The Relationship Between Selected and Nonintellective Factors and Concealed Failures Among College Students of Superior Scholastic Ability," (Unpublished Doctoral Dissertation, Purdue University, 1960), p. 76.

21. Paul Witty and S. W. Bloom, "Science Provisions for the Gifted," Exceptional Children, 1954, p. 244.

22. L. M. Terman, "The Discovery and Encouragement of Exceptional Talent," American Psychologist, 1954, p. 225.

23. B. S. Hollingshead, Who Shall Go To College (New York: Columbia University Press, 1958), p. 24.

24. W. Ralph McCaw, Monarch Notes and Study Guide: Educational Psychology (New York: Monarch Press, Inc., 1969), p. 80.

25. Lucille Bowie and Morgan Gerthon, "Personal Values and Verbal Behavior," Journal of Experimental Education, 1952, p. 338.

26. Joseph S. Junell, "Abolish Letter Grades for Student Teaching Activities," Education, Vol. LXXXIX (March, 1969), p. 225.

27. Albert T. Murphy, "Educational Materials and Individual Psychology," Journal of Education, Vol. CLII (April, 1969), p. 64.

28. F. D. Tikalsky, "Values and Psychological Theory Preferences," (Unpublished Ed.D. Dissertation, Colorado State College, 1966), p. 46.

29. Angelo Dispenzieri and Seymour Giniger, et. al., "College Performance of Disadvantaged Students as a Function of Ability and Personality," Counseling Psychology, Vol. XVIII (July, 1971), p. 298.

30. Patricia S. Plant, "An Experimental Freshmen Program in the Humanities," The Journal of Higher Education, Vol. XXXIX (April, 1968), p. 210.

31. H. H. Hyman, Interviewing in Social Research, (Chicago: University of Chicago Press, 1954), p. 212.

32. Abraham H. Maslow, The Farther Reaches of Human Nature, (New York: The Viking Press, 1973), p. 111.

33. John W. Gardner, Self-Renewal: The Individual and the Innovative Society, (New York: Harper & Row Publishers, 1965), p. 124.

34. Clyde Kluckholn, Culture and Behavior, (New York: The Free Press of Glencoe, 1962), p. 289.

35. Edward D. Eddy, Jr., "Changing Values and Attitudes on Campus," Long Range Planning in Education, (Washington, D.C., American Council on Education, 1959), p. 35.

36. Seth Arsenian, "Changes in Evaluative Attitudes During Four Years of College," Journal of Applied Psychology, 1943, p. 349.

37. Gordon W. Allport and Phillip E. Vernon, A Study of Values, (Boston: Houghton Mifflin Company, 1960), p. 75.

38. Morris E. Eson, _Psychological Foundations of Education_, (New York: Holt, Rinehart and Winston, Inc., 1972), p. 170.

39. Radoslav A. Tsanoff, _The Great Philosophers_, (New York: Harper & Row Publishers, 1964), pp. 138-139.

40. _Ibid._

41. Alfred Marshall, _Principles of Economics_, (New York: The Macmillan Company, 1962), p. 28.

42. Kenneth E. Boulding, _Knowledge in Life and Society: The Image_, Ann Arbor, Michigan: (The University of Michigan Press, 1966), pp. 83-84.

43. Kenneth E. Boulding, _Knowledge in Life and Society: The Image_, (Ann Arbor, Michigan: The University of Michigan Press, 1966), pp. 97-103.

44. Peter A. Bertocci, _Introduction to the Philosophy of Religion_, (New York: Prentice Hall, Inc., 1951), p. 9.

45. Harry S. Broudy, _Building a Philosophy of Education_, (Englewood Cliffs, New Jersey: Prentice Hall, Inc., 1959), pp. 430-447.

46. Franz Alexander, _Psychoanalysis and Psychotherapy_, (New York: W. W. Norton and Company, Inc., 1956), p. 17.

47. _Ibid._

48. Russell Coleburt, _A Precipice of Knowledge_, (New York: Sheed and World, 1957), pp. 25-27.

49. Herbert M. Hamlin, _The Public and Its Education_, (Danville, Illinois: The Interstate Printers and Publishers, 1955), p. 45.

50. Clyde Kluckhohn, _Modern Education and Human Values_, (Pittsburg, Pennsylvania: University of Pittsburg Press, 1952), pp. 87-88.

51. _Ibid._, pp. 129-131.

52. Theodore Brameld, _Ends and Means in Education_, (New York: Harper and Brothers, Publishers, 1950), p. 46.

53. _Op. cit._, p. 68.

54. Maxine Dunfee and Claudia Crump, "Teaching for Social Values in Social Studies," (Washington, D.C., Association for Childhood Education International, 1974), p. 74.

55. John P. Sikula and Others, "Value Changes in Black and White University Interns." A Paper Presented at the Annual Meeting of the American Educational Research, Chicago: Illinois (April, 1974), 1-17.

56. J. Doyle Casteel and Others, "Value Classification in the Social Studies: Six Formats of Value Sheet." Florida Educational Research and Development Council, Gainesville: Florida (July, 1974), 59.

57. Frances E. Hazard, and Charles H. Danner, "Predicting Student Achievement in a

Two-Year Engineering Technology Program." A Paper Presented at the Annual Meeting of North Central States for Community-Junior College Research. A.E.R.A. Chicago, Illinois. (July, 1974).

58. Longitudinal Study and Grade Performance of Students Entering Harper College, Years 1967-1972. Educational Document Reproduction Services. Arlington, Virginia (April, 1974), 5.

59. Kenneth A. Wolkon and Cleveland O. Clarke, "Attitude and Value Change in Minority Teacher Trainees in an Intensive Teacher-Training Program." Educational Document Reproduction Services. Arlington, Virginia (June, 1974), 32.

60. Lewis Karstensson, "A Study on the Validity and Reliability on Student Attitude Toward Economics." Educational Document Reproduction Services, Arlington, Virginia (1972), 57.

61. Janet R. Collins and K. N. Nickel, "A Study of Grading Practices in Institutions of Higher Education." Educational Document Reproduction Services, Arlington, Virginia (1974), p. 18.

62. Paul W. Harris and Others, "Change and Academic Illness: Some Implications for the Prediction of College Grades." Educational Document Reproduction Services, Arlington, Virginia (1973), p. 13.

63. Ann G. Rueben, "Improving Teacher-Student Relationships Through Small Discussion Groups." Educational Document Reproduction Services, Arlington, Virginia (1971), p. 9.

64. John C. Weidman, "The Effects of Academic Departments on Changes in Undergraduates' Occupational Values." National Center for Educational Research and Development. Washington, D.C., 1974, p. 174.

65. Melvyn Ellner, and Arnold Bernstein, "The Frustration-Aggression, Hypothesis and Depression." Educational Document Reproduction Services. Arlington, Virginia, 1973, p. 19.

## Books

Alexander, Franz. Psychoanalysis and Psychotheraphy. New York: W. W. Norton and Company, 1956.

Allport, Gordon W. and Vernon Phillip E. A Study of Values. Boston: Houghton Mifflin Company, 1960.

Anastasti, Anne. Psychological Testing. New York: The Macmillan Company, 1941.

Bernabei, Raymond and Leles, Sam. Behavioral Objectives in Curriculum and Evaluation. Dubuque, Iowa: Kendall-Hunt Publishing Company, 1970.

Bigge, Morris and Hunt, Maurice F. Psychological Foundations of Education. New York: Harper and Row Publishers Company, 1968.

Boulding, Kenneth E. Knowledge in Life and Society. Ann Arbor, Michigan: The University of Michigan Press, 1966.

Brameld, Theodore. Ends and Means in Education. New York: Harper and Row Brothers, 1950.

Broom, Leonard and Others. Sociology. New York: Harper and Row Publishers, Inc., 1959.

Buros, Oscar K. The Sixth Mental Measurement Yearbook. Highland Park, New Jersey: The Gryphon Press, 1965.

Coleburt, Russell. A Precipice of Knowledge. New York: Sheed and Word, 1957.

Combs, Arthur W. and Syngg, Donald. Individual Behavior. New York: Harper and Row Publishers, Inc., 1959.

Eddy, Edward D. "Changing Values and Attitudes on Campus" Long Range Planning in Education. Washington, D.C.: American Council on Education, 1959.

Eson, Morris E. Psychological Foundations of Education. New York: Holt, Rinehart and Winston, Inc., 1972.

Gardner, John W. Self-Renewal: The Individual and the Innovative Society. New York: Harper & Row Publishers, Inc., 1965.

Hamlin, Herbert M. The Public and Its Education. Danville, Illinois: The Interstate Printers and Publishers, 1955.

Hebb, D. O. Textbook of Psychology. Philadelphia, Pennsylvania: W. B. Saunders Company, 1972.

Hollingshead, B. S. Who Should Go to College. New York: Columbia University Press, 1952.

Hyman, H. H. Interviewing in Social Research. Chicago: The University of Chicago Press, 1954.

Kluckhohn, Clyde. Culture and Behavior. New York: The Free Press of Glencoe, 1962.

Lindgreen, Henry C. and Others. Psychology. An Introduction to Behavioral Science. New York: John Wiley and Sons, 1966.

McCaw, Ralph W. Monarch Notes and Study Guide: Educational Psychology. New York: Monarch Press, Inc., 1969.

Marshall, Alfred. Principles of Economics. New York: The Macmillan Company, 1962.

Maslow, Abraham H. The Farther Reaches of Human Nature. New York: The Viking Press, 1973.

Morris, Charles G. Psychology: An Introduction. New York: Appleton-Century-Crofts, 1973.

Munn, Normal L. The Fundamentals of Human Adjustment. Boston: Houghton Mifflin Company, 1966.

Sanford, Fillmore H. Psychology: A Scientific Study of Man. Belmont, California: Wadsworth Publishing Company, 1967.

Tsanoff, Radoslav A. The Great Philosophers. New York: Harper and Row Publishers, Inc., 1964.

Van Dalen, Deobold and Meter, William T. Understanding Educational Research. New York: McGraw-Hill, Inc., 1966.

Williams, Rubin M., Jr. American Society: A Sociological Interpretation. New York: Knopf Publishing Company, 1960.

## Periodical Articles

Arsenian, Seth. "Changes in Evaluative Attitudes During Four Years of College." Journal of Applied Psychology (1943), 349.

Barr, A. S. "Recruitment of Teacher Training and Prediction of Teacher Success." Review of Educational Research. No. 10 (1940), 185-193.

Bowie, Lucille and Gerthon, Morgan. "Personal Values and Verbal Behavior." Journal of Experimental Education. No. 30 (1952), 337-341.

Dispenzieri, Angelo and Giniger, Seymour and Others. "College Performance of Disadvantaged Students as a Function of Ability and Personality." Counseling Psychology. Vol. 28 (1971), 298.

Hill, Robert E., Jr. "Scholastic Success of College Freshmen from Parochial and Public Secondary Schools." The School Review (1961), 48-60.

Junell, Joseph S. "Abolish Letter Grades for Student Activities." Education. Vol. 89 (1969), 225.

Murphy, Albert T. "Educational Materials and Individual Psychology." Journal of Education. Vol. 152 (1969), p. 64.

Plant, Patricia S. "An Experimental Freshmen Program in the Humanities." The Journal of Higher Education. Vol. 39 (1968), 210.

Terman, L. M.  "The Discovery and Encouragement of Exceptional Talent."  American Psychologist.  (1954), 244.

Witty, Paul and Bloom, S. W.  "Science Provisions for the Gifted."  Exceptional Children.  (1954), 244.

## Unpublished Dissertations

Bond, Patricia J.  "The Relationship Between Selected and Non-Intellective Factors and Concealed Failures Among College Students of Superior Scholastic Ability."  Unpublished Doctoral Dissertation, Purdue University, Lafayette, Indiana.  1960.

Brady, William J.  "Twenty Quantitative Predictors of Academic Success as Measured by Grade Point Averages."  Unpublished Doctoral Dissertation, University of Connecticut, Storrs, Connecticut, 1965.

Johnson, Joseph R.  "A History of Millersbury Institute."  Unpublished Doctoral Dissertation, Laurence University, Sarasota, Florida, 1971.

Tikalsky, F. D.  "Values and Psychological Theory Preference."  Unpublished Ed.D. Dissertation, Colorado State College, Fort Collins, Colorado, 1966.

## Research Documents

Casteel, J. Doyle and Others.  "Value Classification in the Social Studies:  Five Formats of Value Sheet."  Research Bulletin.  Florida Educational Research and Development Council, Gainesville.  July, 1974, p. 9.

Collins, Janet R. and Nickel, K. N.  "A Study of Grading Practices in Institutions of Higher Education."  Educational Document Reproduction Services, Arlington, Virginia.  1974, p. 18.

Dugan, Ruth R. and Others.  "A Comparative Study of Anxieties Among Current (1972) Glassboro State College Freshmen and Their Counterparts of 1964."  Educational Document Research Services.  Arlington, Virginia.  1973, p. 38.

Dunfee, Maxine and Crump, Claudia.  "Teaching for Social Values in Social Studies."  Association for Childhood Educational International.  Washington, D.C. 1974, p. 74.

Ellner, Melvyn and Bernstein, Arnold.  "The Frustration-Aggression Hypothesis and Depression."  Educational Document Research Services.  Arlington, Virginia.  1973, p. 19.

Harris, Paul W. and Others.  "Change and Academic Illness:  Some Implications for the Predictions of College Grades."  Educational Document Research Services.  Arlington, Virginia.  1973, p. 13.

Hazard, Frances E. and Danner, Charles H.  "Predicting Student Achievement in Two-year Engineering Technology Program."  A paper presented at the annual meeting of North Central States AERA/SIG for Community Junior College Research.  July, 1974.

Karstensson, Lewis.  "A Study of the Validity and Reliability of a Questionnaire on Student Attitude Toward Economics."  Educational Document Reproduction Services.  Arlington, Virginia.  1972, p. 57.

Longitudinal Study and Grade Performance of Students Entering Harper College - Years
1967-1972. Educational Document Reproduction Services. Arlington, Virginia.
1974, p. 5.

Ruben, Ann G. "Improving Teacher-Student Relationships Through Small Discussion
Groups." Educational Document Reproduction Services. Arlington, Virginia,
1971, p. 9.

Sikula, John P. and Others. "Value Changes in Black and White University Interns."
A paper presented at the annual meeting of American Educational Research Association. Chicago, Illinois. April 15-19, 1974, p. 17.